"History is a nightmare from which I am trying to awake."
James Joyce

"History is a mysterious approach to closeness."
Martin Buber

Burning Children
A Jewish View of the War in Gaza

This book and other titles by Marc H. Ellis may be ordered through local booksellers or by contacting:

New Diaspora Books

e - **info**@newdiasporabooks.com · w - www.**newdiasporabooks**.com

---

Burning Childeren: A Jewish View of the War in Gaza
is part of Marc H. Ellis's *Exile and the Prophetic* featured at mondoweiss.net

ISBN:978-0-9907609-0-0

Cover Photograph
Ezz Al Zanoon

Feature Photographs
*Ahmad, Ryan Rodrick Beiler, Kelly Lynn, Marc H. Ellis,
Tim B. Gilman, Max Blumenthal, The Jewish Journal, auschwitz.org, Wikipedia*

Design
timmyroland.com

*To all those who witness at the the end
of Jewish history as we have known and inherited it.*

NEW**DIASPORA**
B O O K S

New Di-as-por-a., n.

***archaic* 1)** the scattering of the Jews to countries outside of Palestine after the Babylonian captivity. **2)** (often. l.c.) the body of Jews living in countries outside of Palestine or modern Israel **3)** such countries collectively: *the return of the Jews from the Diaspora.*

***of recent origin* 4)** political, cultural and religious exiles who gather **5)** forming a community without borders **6)** to witness to life abundant: *a community that honors the shattered fragments of diverse cultural heritages and faith commitments* **7)** intending those fragments to be shared with fellow exiles without the desire to recreate an idolatrous whole: *not excluding the shattered concept of worship and God that has contributed so much discrimination, violence and genocide to the world* **8)** such a community is bound together by the prophetic expressed in diverse linguistic and symbolic formations **9)** so that the exilic journey will be characterized by fidelity and thus not be in vain: *thereby bequeathing justice-seeking, compassion and the search for meaning to future generations.*

BURNING CHILDREN

A **JEWISH** VIEW OF THE WAR IN GAZA

MARC H. ELLIS

TABLE OF CONTENTS

INTRODUCTION

For many years I have been writing on Jewish identity, the Holocaust, Israel and Palestine. Throughout, I have been searching for a way out of the violence that has engulfed Palestinians and Jews.

During these years, there have been times of reckoning, times when the world watched and wondered. Could this go on forever?

With the Gaza war we have arrived at another reckoning. We cannot afford to let this moment pass without a change of heart – and direction.

The suffering of Palestinians is extreme. Israel's denial of Palestinian statehood has consequences. One of them is violence seemingly without end. Caught in that violence are mostly civilians – many of them children.

As I write, the death toll in Gaza has reached two thousand dead with thousands more injured. How many more will die until Palestinians are free in their own homeland?

I write as a Jew on behalf of Jews of Conscience in America, in Israel and around the world.

Jews of Conscience want to live a life of integrity and justice in light of our own history. Jews are known for our forced wandering and persecution - and for our pursuit of justice. Jews cannot rest easy when others suffer because of us.

From the time three Israeli youth went missing in June 2014, through Israel's subsequent invasion of Gaza in July and August, I wrote commentary for Mondoweiss, an online journal that explores the difficulties and possibilities of Israel-Palestine.

My series title, "Exile and the Prophetic," suggests the position of Jews of Conscience in exile from the mainstream Jewish community struggling to practice the indigenous of Jewish life, the prophetic. In these commentaries I ask myself, other Jews and people of good will what is to be done to create a future of justice and reconciliation for Jews and Palestinians.

For if we as Jews come after the Holocaust, we also come after Israel and what Jews have done and are doing to the Palestinian people. What does it mean to be faithful as a Jew after the Holocaust and after Israel?

For Christians and Muslims in solidarity with Jews and Palestinians, the road is far from easy. Charges of anti-Semitism lurk in the background and the difficulties Jews have faced in history are cautionary. Nonetheless, Israel has gone off the rails in its violence. Israel's violence in occupation and war must be stopped.

No desire for security can explain the crimes Israel has committed in Gaza.

The title of this book comes from the writings of Rabbi Irving Greenberg, an Orthodox Jew and a leading Holocaust theologian. Referring to the burning children of the Holocaust many years ago, Rabbi Greenberg wrote: "After the Holocaust, no statement, theological or otherwise, should be made that would not be credible in the presence of burning children."

The challenge of burning children of the Holocaust is so monumental that Greenberg, again as an Orthodox rabbi, suggests a non-theological response: "The act of creating a life or enhancing its dignity is the counter-testimony to Auschwitz. To talk of love and of a God who cares in the presence of the burning children is obscene and incredible; to leap in and pull a child out of a pit, to clean its face and heal its body, is to make the most powerful statement – the only statement that counts."

During Israel's invasion of Gaza, Jews of Conscience responded to Rabbi Greenberg's plea. That the burning children of today are Palestinian suffering at the hands of Jews represents one of the great reversals in the annals of history. Where once Jewish fidelity was defined as support for Israel, today saving burning Palestinian children has become the touchstone of Jewish fidelity.

Rather than a history or a political primer on the Israeli-Palestinian conflict, in these pages I highlight various dimensions of Israel's invasion of Gaza. But the central question throughout is how to move Jews in Israel and around the world to see that Jews can only be free if Palestinians are free as well. During the Gaza war we could not be further from this goal. This makes it even more imperative that we begin anew now.

I leave these commentaries as they were written – in the heat of battle. What will happen in the coming days and months will be telling and demand further thought and clarification. Without knowing the outcome in advance, I think these thoughts are timely. They may help us ponder a future different then the war we have just lived through.

Gilad Sha'ar, Naftali Frenke, Eyal Yifrah
Murdered Israeli Teenagers

MISSING!

The skies are once again darkening over Palestine. As if it wasn't dark enough. With three Israeli teenagers missing and presumed kidnapped, Israel has unleashed its usual backlash against Palestinians. It's overkill. Time to teach Palestinians yet another lesson on who is the boss.

The days ahead promise more of the same and, God forbid, the teenagers aren't found alive, it's anyone's guess what will happen then. The problem as always is the power disparity and the occupation itself. But in the rush to judgment all of that is left behind. The issue becomes the kidnapping of the innocent.

In occupation, the innocent suffer. Can it only be Palestinians who suffer? There is a cost to occupation. Even the powerful have to pay a price. Jews have to pay a price – when they're occupiers.

Missing Jews are a terrible price to pay. But, then, Israeli jails are filled with "missing" Palestinians.

As usual, the ratio of missing Jews and Palestinians is telling. No one wants to compare the missing – every missing person is a horror – but again the disparity is telling. Does this disparity signal the presumed worthiness of Jewish and Palestinian lives?

Missing too are Jewish ethics in Israel and elsewhere. The outrage about missing Jews – if it was only matched for missing Palestinians. One looks in vain for this outrage. Which itself is an outrage.

The shared intelligence, the Palestinian Authority's willingness to devote its resources to find the missing Israelis, is commendable. If truth be told, however, the Palestinian Authority's energy would be better spent searching for it's own soul. That soul seems to be missing too.

Perhaps both could be done at the same time: searching for the teenagers and telling Israel to back out of its territory, never to return.

So return the missing – on all sides. Including the land and ethics and service to one's own people.

When all the missing are returned then we could begin again. A fresh start, honoring all the missing, which, in justice, would be returned.

IDF Moves In
West Bank

KIDNAPPED

The hunt continues for the missing Israeli teenagers. The roundup of Palestinians also continues. More than 150 Palestinians have already been taken by Israel's military. Have they, too, been kidnapped?

Interesting that the Israelis taken were on their way back from settlements where they study at yeshivas. I haven't had a chance to look at the various course catalogs but I assume the yeshivas don't specialize in interfaith dialogue. I doubt these yeshivas have majors in the Abrahamic faith traditions or cutting-edge programs in interfaith relations.

Yeshivas in the West Bank aren't into Martin Buber.

The religion of the occupiers is always an imperialist one. Can it be any different for Judaism when its practitioners occupy another people?

The West Bank, and especially Hebron, is once again cordoned off and invaded by the Israeli military. In the situation of occupation, Jews traveling into and out of the West Bank are committing political acts.

This doesn't mean that kidnapping is the civilized way of registering grievances. However, since the war against Palestinians is so devastating and ongoing, the weapons used by the weak cannot be dictated by the powerful.

Like suicide bombing, kidnapping is the weapon of the weak. One doesn't have to condone such actions to understand this reality.

Israel isn't a civilized occupier. In the way it acts toward Palestinians, Israel isn't civilized at all. Israel kidnaps Palestinians on a regular basis – including Palestinian government officials. For Israel, it is exercising a self-evident right. To dominate another people?

Secretary of State John Kerry is up in arms: How dare they! Yet the American record of invasion and yes – kidnapping – isn't one to fall back on. This is where we are as the Presbyterian debate on divestment begins. It's an important moment but against this darkening military backdrop everyone knows important symbolism sometimes carries very little bite.

Perhaps the Presbyterians ought to be kidnapped. Someone should take hold of their minds and (portfolio) wallets. The largesse of their portfolio and their capitalist timidity to dole out anything but a pittance is a scandal.

Alms in the name of Jesus?

This is where we are. We have been here for decades. Stuck – with dire consequences.

Searching Everywhere
West Bank

HUNTING
FOR MISSING JUSTICE

Here we go again. Israel has launched – yet another – full-scale invasion of the West Bank. This in response to the kidnapping of three Israelis. Or is this a cover for – yet another – collective punishment because the Palestinians declared – yet again – a Palestinian state?

Allison Deger is on the scene covering this amazing story. It seems that Palestine is that unique type of state that keeps declaring itself, is continually invaded with impunity and where the state's government is expected to and even volunteers to cooperate with the invaders.

Still, folks like Larry Derfner, in an interesting appeal to liberal Zionists, and after detailing why everything else has failed, thinks that BDS has a chance of succeeding. It's a last ditch effort to be sure and Derfner thinks that at most there is 10 years left to try it. But what the heck, the Jewish state is worth saving. Just do it!

Here's Derfner:

> Not even Ben-Gurion would be able to rally the political support necessary to displace masses of settlers as long as there is no price to be paid for the occupation. So how much longer can liberal Zionists sit and watch the status quo remain static? If instead of trying to persuade Israel to change, two-state supporters started holding it responsible for refusing to change, it could have a jarring psychological impact on the country and its leaders.

The question answered is simply put: Not even up-in-arms BDS-active liberal Zionists can save the day for a – real – two-state solution.

The truth of the matter is that as the divestment debate is upon us, what's left of Palestine is doubly occupied by the Palestinian Authority and Israeli soldiers.

I am beginning to wonder whether the Palestinian Authority wants the responsibility of governing an intact, contiguous, real, Palestinian state. If that was in the cards, the political skill needed would be unparalleled. Do the Palestinian Authority and Hamas prefer the Israeli occupation with American brokering some kind of autonomy as their solution to the mirage of difficulties that would accompany Palestinian freedom?

Here's Mahmoud Abbas yesterday on the subject of cooperation with Israel:

> It's in our interest that there is security coordination between us and Israel in order to protect ourselves, to protect our people. We do not want to go back to the anarchy or destruction that happened in the second intifada

Abbas's statement seems to confirm what Abdullah Al-Majali points out about the culpability of the Palestinian Authority:

> When it comes to Zionists, all forms of logic are disregarded and the world is turned upside down: right becomes wrong and wrong becomes right; justice becomes injustice and injustice becomes justice; the victim is seen as the oppressor and the oppressor is seen as the victim; the kidnapped becomes the kidnapper while the kidnapper becomes the kidnapped.

> In every stage of history, there is a force that determines moral standards and adjusts them according to its own moral compass. Today, though, we see Palestinian officials sharing our blood assuming a moral code closer to the Zionists' standards rather than the truth and justice believed in by their own people.

Everything is upside down and we have to put it right side up again. The situation as it is makes turning things right side almost impossible. The young Jewish – students with an imperialist take on Judaism and Jewishness – have been kidnapped.

They're missing in the Zionist / Israeli / Jewish universe. But when the search assaults an entire nation, we have to turn our attention elsewhere.

To justice.

Going Door to Door
Aida Refugee Camp

AFTER THE CELEBRATION:
KIDNAPPING AND ASSAULTING
AN ENTIRE NATION

The victory for divestment in the Presbyterian biannual convention last night is being widely heralded and rightly so. The work of many Christians – and Jews – over the years is finally coming to fruition. So celebration is in order. Now the political work has to begin again.

The political challenge at the moment is captured vividly by a YWCA – Palestine Action Alert published in conjunction with the divestment vote. The alert is sobering. It's also a wake-up call.

Israel's invasion of the already occupied West Bank continues. The title *"Assaulting and Kidnapping Our Future"* is apt and more. The alert defines the issue before us:

> There is much talk and violent responses to the abduction of three Israeli youth. Although we join with others in our condemnation of all abductions, yet the raids of cities and towns and refugee camps and siege over a whole population by the Israeli army calls on us to act. The West Bank is under a full scale siege which includes hundreds of raids and assaults on homes, media stations, refugee camps, and even charitable societies. At this moment over 370 people have been kidnapped and detained including members of Hamas, members of Parliament, and released prisoners from the Shalit exchange. Three young people have been killed and at least 7 critically injured. Roads and checkpoints are closed and work permits are being ripped up. In addition, Israel bombs Gaza "targets" nightly. A three month year old baby was killed last night. This is what it means to live under military occupation and what is meant by the term "collective punishment."

The Palestinian Human Rights Organizations Council (PHROC) condemns Israel's reprisals against the Palestinian population in carrying out its investigations of the disappeared settler youths and demands Israel to abide by the Geneva conventions.

We also believe that all of Palestinian society has been kidnapped. Every time a soldier enters a Palestinian home in the middle of the night and with violence threatens or takes away a brother, a sister, a father, or a mother this is kidnapping. In addition, there are 5,271 prisoners in Israeli jails with hundreds under "administrative detention." Their lives and their family's lives have been kidnapped. This military siege and all its many forms is more than "collective punishment"; it is violence against Palestinian women and their families on a grand scale. It deserves our prayers and our actions to stop it.

This alert's language is concise –"We also believe that all of Palestinian society has been kidnapped"– and is much stronger than the Presbyterian's often repeated assurance last night that their divestment vote was a form of love for "both our Israeli and Palestinian brothers and sisters." For when "our brothers and sisters" are being assaulted, symbolic action has to be complemented by direct action.

But then the alert's suggestions for action, while instructive, are limited. We all know they won't be applied.

- Pray for our families in all the refugee camps and all the traumatized children through the West Bank and Gaza.

- Hold Israel accountable for these gross violations of international law including SCR 1325 that demands protection of women;

- Send letters to your MPs, representatives, or Foreign Affair Ministers to demand that the attacks end;

- Pressure your governments to continue to seek a just Peace for both Palestinians and Israelis, and for the implementation of all UN resolutions pertaining to Palestine, so all peoples can live in peace and security.

This is where we are. As a nation is being kidnapped and assaulted once again, even our most dedicated activists are handcuffed by the reality unfolding before the world's eyes.

So many thoughts on the divestment vote are worthy of comment. Watching the streamed discussion at the convention was instructive, invigorating and sobering – often at the same time. But the deeper exploration of the Presbyterian divestment affair awaits another day. Right now the same energy expended on divestment should be applied to the politics that allow Israel to invade Palestine at will.

Reversing the occupation. Where the activists' rubber meets the apartheid road.

Advocating for Divestment
Detroit

VICTORY'S
UNINTENDED CONSEQUENCES

It isn't time for an evaluation of the recent victory among Presbyterians in the BDS struggle. After all, the after-glow of victory should be enjoyed for at least a week or two. But the kidnapping of the Jewish teenagers and the subsequent invasion of the West Bank has cast a pall over everything bright and sunny.

Time passes all too quickly in the disenchanted (un) Holy Land that stretches between Tel Aviv and the Jordan River. Who even remembers John Kerry's solve-the-issue-once-and-for-all peace plan that dissolved only months ago?

The commentators are having a field day on the Presbyterian divestment vote. Most are rehashing the same scenario but it seems that a major point is absent from the discussion. The unintended consequences of the BDS victory a few days ago may move in a very different direction than the winners hoped for.

Victory is a victory and, though a squeaker, the Presbyterians did vote for divestment from three companies that profit from the occupation of Palestinians. But to say that the Presbyterians have signed on to divestment is disingenuous.

Two years ago the Presbyterians narrowly defeated a similar measure. We can be sure that the issue will be revisited at the next assembly in 2016. Like many Christian denominations, the Presbyterians are split down the middle on the issue.

But the divestment victory has come at a cost. The cost is simply put. If you look at the hem's and haw's of the passed resolution and the comments by Presbyterian officials during and after the vote, the victory is parsed as a supportive measure for a just Israel as, in the Presbyterian's view, Israel was and could be again. Support for Palestinians, while stated, is secondary. The love expressed toward our "brother and sister" Israelis and Palestinians is further subordinated to the relationships that the Presbyterians have cultivated with American Jews.

If all politics is local, the local Rabbi is much more important and closer to most Presbyterians than the local Imam or Palestinian – if either is even in the neighborhood. Another way of putting it: Israel is all over the Presbyterian prayer cycle; Mohammed and Islam aren't.

The unintended consequences of the Presbyterian vote are important. They include drawing closer than ever to Israel as a Jewish state precisely when the BDS movement is questioning the very possibility of such an Israel embracing a just peace with the Palestinian people. By divesting from three corporations, the Presbyterians affirmed once again the two-state solution and, at the same time, excused from culpability other corporations who benefit directly or indirectly from profiting in the occupation. In actuality, this means any corporation doing business with Israel since in one way or another almost every Israeli corporation participates in and benefits financially from the occupation.

At the same time, the Presbyterians drew the line on BDS. They were explicit: In no way is their action to be interpreted to show support for the BDS movement. At least implicitly, they support the view that one of BDS's goals is to undermine the legitimacy of the state of Israel.

Again, a victory is a victory. But if I were in the Israeli government I would think twice about pouting. Unlike the Presbyterians, Israel has an army which it was using as the votes were tallied. The re-invasion of the West Bank is telling as are the limits of the Presbyterians on what really counts in the ongoing – and intensifying – struggle in Israel-Palestine.

When the chips are down, the Presbyterians are on Israel's side. As they have been.

At this point, what more could Israel ask for?

Rabbi Lynn Gottlieb & Lubna
Bethlehem

The Rationality
of Israel's War

In a Facebook comment about a photo of burning rubble accompanying the Israeli bombing of Gaza after the death of the three kidnapped Israelis was confirmed, the longtime justice activist, Rabbi Lynn Gottlieb, posed this question:

> *Is the death of more innocents really the answer to the killing of Naftali, Eyal and Gilad? More families mourning, more homes destroyed, more outrage, bitterness and despair?*

Rabbi Gottlieb's question is right on.

Her answer – "Militarism is insanity incarnate"– is wrong.

Here lies the rub.

Militarism isn't irrational at all – from the perspective of those who benefit from it. War isn't a waste either – from the perspective of those who benefit from it.

It could be that those who think they benefit from militarism and war are wrong. They're just fooling themselves. The reply of the powerful, however, is heard around the globe: "If it's true that history isn't kind to anyone for very long, why not live it up now by dominating others?"

What goes around eventually comes around. Does that mean that the powerful should limit their power today because one day it will come back to haunt them? Perhaps. Few in power think this way. Should they?

Boomerang is interesting as a metaphor. What happens in history is real. Over time history is sorted out; interpretation is high drama. However, reality on the ground is defined by power.

21

If ethics and morality have a say in history, it's too late in coming.

Some Palestinians still wager on others, including Israel, to do the right thing. These Palestinians should be honored for their deep humanity and perseverance. They should also have their heads examined.

The same is true with conspiracy theorists peddling stories about what "really" happened to the three Israelis. Were the three kidnapped and by whom? If they were taken, was it Hamas, paid informers, the Mossad? Did Israel set it all up?

Like the boomerang effect, conspiracies have their place. The kidnapping and murder certainly could be a set-up, though it would take gamesmanship of the highest order. Like Ariel Sharon but with much better English, Benjamin Netanyahu is a plodder. Events have fallen into his lap, as has happened throughout Israel's history. To attribute conspiratorial heroism to Netanyahu is foolhardy.

Since Palestinians and their supporters have been unable to understand how America and the world have let Israel get away with ethnic cleansing, land theft, settlements, the various invasions of Lebanon, Gaza and alike, the Apartheid Wall – the list is endless – conspiracy theories have a life of their own.

Other than (the obviously silent and absent) God, the defeated have little else to hold onto.

To enter into the world of conspiracy is to take rational thought down a path where critical thinking becomes impossible. Conspiracy theorists become mirror images of their oppressors. Except the oppressors have power.

Israel doesn't need conspiracies, even if they concoct and use them.

The other side of conspiracy theory is a world where everything becomes symbolism.

As the Presbyterians voted to profit from other unjust corporations than the ones they divested from, Israel was already on the military prowl. Celebrations of the divestment victory went deep into the night. The internet is full of congratulatory messages despite the blowback and the limitations of the divestment vote itself.

The miscalculation was extreme. Like a young halfback, Israel ran down field with the divestment symbolism securely tucked underneath its' arm. There wasn't a tackler with any heft in sight.

Yet another conspiracy?

What to do when the field of real battle is so one-sided is the only question worth asking now. There aren't any easy answers.

Militarism may be misguided from a certain point of view. Conspiracy theories and symbolism have their place. But Israel, along with any country that holds its own militarily, knows that when the chips are down or the opportunities arise the boomerang down the road and the conspiracy theory up ahead – with periodic symbolic defeats – aren't worth much. They may even help the powerful accomplish their goals.

The insanity of militarism that Rabbi Gottlieb writes about is for justice seekers who mourn what the powerful don't give a damn about.

Israel isn't pondering the insanity of militarism. Why should it?

Along the Via Dolorosa
Jerusalem

REAL & SURREAL
IN OCCUPIED PALESTINE

From a correspondent in Jerusalem:

> *Life is surreal. I am sitting in the educational bookstore listening to lovely Arab music answering emails with the sound of helicopters overhead and old men sauntering by coming from the Al Aqsa with prayer rugs on their heads to protect them from the sun.*

That's often the reality of occupations, incursions, invasions, wars – ordinary life and extraordinary violence. The combination is surreal.

In Israel/Palestine, it's a way of life. Either heading toward, tapering off or beginning another round in other ways. The surreal mix is heady, dangerous and violent. The surreal is real.

We were supposed to be at the end. So John Kerry said. As many did before. But this was it, final, all claims settled, a new reality on the ground.

Meaning what? To whom?

Now we are on the brink of another wave of violence, or in the middle of a new wave. Isn't it one long arc of violence of which this is the latest?

Thinking about settler violence, settler rampages, settler murders. The call from political authorities, including Prime Minister Netanyahu, to pipe down, show restraint, act civilized is disingenuous while the soldiers under his command invade and bomb, blow up homes and shoot children.

What type of violence is worse – mob violence or state violence?

The combination is the cruelest as we Jews know well. Now Jews are involved in a similar way. We remember, at least we should, that the quelling of mob violence was the prelude to the greater violence to come.

The lessons of history have been lost to us. Or did we learn them too well?

Here from the YWCA - Palestine that deadly combination - on the ground as events are unfolding:

> Helicopters buzz overhead all day. Tear gas chokes the air around the Shu'fat Refugee camp as youth with stones clash with soldiers in response to more murders. Near Beit Hanina the roads are closed or blocked. "Death to Arabs" was the rally cry of thousands on Jaffa Street last night seeking a lynching after the funeral of the three Israeli youth who were found dead in shallow graves on June 29th. This is on top of the burning of the homes of the families of the suspected killers in Hebron and the nightly bombings in Gaza.

> Two more Palestinian youth were murdered in Shu'fat Refugee camp near Jerusalem— one was burned to death. We are trying to keep up with the death toll during this state sanctified reign of terror. Whole communities are in lock down or under military control while the rest of us are reliving past traumas or memories of intifadas. Israel's rampage is not a response to terror nor is it a military sweep or manhunt as it also includes paramilitary settlers who act and murder with impunity.

Star of David helicopter gunships and settlers rampaging. I wonder what color shirts they're wearing? I doubt it's Nazi brown. Star of David blue?

You see when the mob comes and the state is there, too, it doesn't matter what color shirts the violent wear. Or what the state is called.

It all comes down to the same thing, even in the "Jewish" state.

Heading for Gaza
Israel

ISRAEL'S WAR
IS JUST BEGINING AND HAS NEVER ENDED

Is it time for commentary on Israel's war that is just beginning and has never ended?

Perhaps.

The airwaves are full of pumped up pro-Israel armchair warriors. It's also full of moral outrage on behalf of Palestinians. A virtual war. Don't be distracted. The real war isn't on TV or Facebook. The real war is on the ground. The days and weeks ahead are going to be brutal.

No mercy will be allowed. War is like that.

As per usual, America has Israel's back. Egypt does too. The United Nations has much more bark than bite. Israel has a free hand.

The hope for change, well, it hasn't arrived. Not even close.

Some refer to the rockets from Gaza as "resistance missiles." Nice touch. But Israeli warplanes hitting targets in Gaza and soldiers gathering on Gaza's borders are the real deal.

Netanyahu wants to finish Hamas off as part of his legacy. Or is it his intention to set Hamas back enough to keep it in place?

As for Secretary of State John Kerry, now you have it – the predictable, logical and official end of your vaunted final, settle all claims peace process.

On the moral outrage and appeal to humanity front, save it. We've been through this countless times. The world is even deafer today than it was when outrage was first ramped up during Israel's various military adventurers in the 1980s. Lebanon and the first Palestinian uprising are distant memories. The lessons weren't learned. The openings weren't taken.

Action alerts and appeals for a ceasefire are important to produce and distribute. Even so, Israel will stop when it's in Israel's interest to stop. Not before.

As for the notion that Gaza is Israel's quagmire, somewhat like America in Vietnam, try a different angle. Gaza is Israel's military testing ground. Tried and true. Always available.

Depressing for those of us watching Israel's war machine once again exert its control? Worse for those who are being targeted. Much worse.

The days ahead, blood and more blood. And more blood beyond that.

Streets of the Ghetto
Warsaw, Poland

WHERE WAS GOD
IN THE WARSAW GHETTO? OR IN GAZA?

Is there a theological lesson in the ongoing bombing and perhaps soon to be invasion of Gaza? The West Bank has already been invaded – and looted. With scores of "kidnapped" prisoners to boot.

Rumors of a US brokered ceasefire have surfaced. This would bring back John Kerry and his crew. Not to mention the recycled Israeli and Palestinian negotiators. What a horrible lot!

Freezing the status quo is in Israel's interest. Damage done. Negotiating starts up again from the new facts on the ground.

With the ongoing war, whatever the shape it takes in the coming days, theology is a side issue or even irrelevant to most observers. But for those who for some inexplicable reason are drawn to God – without making any claims for that unrequited condition – the matter of God is most serious.

To sum it up politely, it doesn't look good for God.

Many years ago I cut my teeth on the question of God in history via the Holocaust and Richard Rubenstein's classic book, *After Auschwitz*. Rubenstein wrote of God's silence and absence, or worse, knowledge and inaction, during the Holocaust. Because of my immersion in the Holocaust world, I think Palestinians and their supporters who await God's intervention are barking up the wrong cosmic tree.

Irony of ironies, Palestinians should pay close attention to the Jewish theological obsession with God's silence, even as they are invaded and bombed by the heirs of the Holocaust.

I also think that Jews should pay close attention to Palestinian suffering and its relation to the question of God. That intense and repeated suffering is being visited upon Palestinians in the name of the Jewish people, the Holocaust and the Jewish God is a reversal of epic proportions.

Without question but rarely identified as such, Israel's continuing injustice and oppression is a formative event in Jewish life that parallels the Holocaust in importance. Thoughts about God today come after Auschwitz and after what Israel has done and is doing to the Palestinian people.

Jews already have a strained relationship with God. That relationship cannot escape the ramifications of Israel's violence.

Think of Israel's bombing of Gaza as the coda on the question of what Jews can think about God after Auschwitz. We can't go back to God. We can't go ahead with God either.

Palestinian religious supporters around the world, among them many religious Muslims and Christians, along with a handful of religious Jews – whatever language and imagery they employ to call on God and their governments – should likewise take note of God's silence. When their prayer vigils end, effective action is minimal.

Should prayer services for the victims of Israel's violence thus be halted?

Yesterday a good friend of mine, who wants to remain anonymous, responded to a question about the lack of response from other countries on behalf of Palestinians. Where are they in this latest flare up of the Israeli-Palestinian war? My friend's response:

> *Theological rule of thumb – to be observed and thought through: Every person (and country) looks out for their own interests. Call it political original sin. No one outside benefits from siding with Palestine in real terms. The sacrifice is too great. Some Palestinians don't side with Palestine either – in their concrete actions. What would happen to the Palestinian governmental and economic elites, for example, if Palestine became free? This is where theology starts from.*

Political original sin? Self-interest isn't only personal. What my friend suggests is that despite the rhetoric, the best appeal is one that materially enhances who you appeal to. This is better than the rhetoric of sacrifice for others. Despite the religiosity around sacrifice, few embrace sacrifice as a way of life.

Have we strayed from the question of God? Not really. You see the silence of God in Gaza is akin to the silence of God in Auschwitz – in the following way: A defenseless people are under assault by a powerful military for the sole reason of further subjugating them. Of course, all sorts of other reasons are offered and, yes, the analogy isn't exact. President Abbas was rightly criticized for suggesting when he asked apropos of the Gaza bombings: "Shall we recall Auschwitz?"

Or was Abbas cutting too close to the Jewish bone?

True, the situation of Jews then and Palestinians now is not exactly the same. So if it helps focus our minds perhaps best to substitute the Warsaw Ghetto for the Auschwitz death camp.

Where was God in the Warsaw Ghetto? Does ramping down the analogy help the Israeli government and Jewish establishment in America breathe a sigh of relief?

Predictably the response to Abbas was swift and certain. Noteworthy is the response from Abraham Foxman, director of the Anti-Defamation League:

> *This is unacceptable language and accusations coming from the leader of the Palestinian Authority. We are used to the outrageous criticisms of Israel coming from Palestinians, but President Abbas has reached a new low in calling Israel's self-defense action, after hundreds of rockets have been launched at Israeli civilians, a "genocide," and then by going even further by comparing Israel's actions to the murder of 1.5 million Jews at Auschwitz.*
>
> *Mr. Abbas is frequently referred to as a "moderate" Palestinian leader, and many still hold out hope that this is true. At a time*

when the Middle East is overrun with extremism in places like Syria and Iraq, to have the leader of the Palestinian Authority further inflame the region with these outrageous comments, is disappointing and dangerous.

We call on the United States, the European Union and other responsible governments to clearly, forcefully and unequivocally denounce these outrageous statements from President Abbas.

This is where we have arrived politically and ethically. Foxman is a Holocaust survivor and a prime enabler of Israeli violence. He doesn't hesitate to lecture Abbas on the Holocaust of history *and* how different (and lesser) the ongoing suffering of the Palestinian people really is.

Actually, rather than a statement, Abbas posed a question. Is it wrong for Palestinians and Jews to recall Auschwitz in the invasion and bombing of defenseless people by the self-proclaimed Jewish state?

Memory is like that. The suffering of one when perpetrated by the former sufferer is likely to bring historical memories to the fore – on both sides.

Theologically speaking it seems that Foxman and the Israeli government, with its many supporters, are announcing God's vengeance on the Palestinians of the West Bank and Gaza. The sins of the Palestinians are variously defined. The main sin of Palestinians seems to be resisting their demise and asserting their dignity. How dare they!

You don't have to go as far as Auschwitz or even the Warsaw Ghetto to appreciate – and support – the Palestinian struggle. Or use the historical memory of Jewish suffering to make your point.

When it comes to God, it's more or less the same story. While Jews, Christians and Muslims believe in a God who intervenes in history, the better part of our belief is that once upon a time God did so – and decisively.

Thus we are left to contemplate the memory of a God who wasn't silent as God in Gaza and beyond is today.

IDF Keeping Watch
Jerusalem

CEASEFIRE.
TIGHTENING THE GORDIAN KNOT?

Yet another ceasefire? The people of Gaza need it badly. But what Gaza needs badly isn't the only or best option in the long run.

Maybe that's why Hamas is a reluctant ceasefire partner.

Of course, the people of Gaza don't have much to say in the matter. If they did, no doubt they'd take a ceasefire in a Gaza heartbeat. If I was living in Gaza I would.

Because there isn't another way out or so it seems. No one in the world with any power is offering anything more than more of the same. A ceasefire means we're back to square one.

But to write that Gaza – without highlighting Jerusalem and the West Bank – is a Gordian Knot as Nervana Mahmoud does is to miss the point. Mahmoud concentrates on the present as if it will determine the future. Perhaps unintentionally, she makes the issue of Israeli occupation and control of Palestinian borders intractable by placing them in the background.

The Palestinian situation is longstanding and dire. Intractable it isn't.

Like most observers, Mahmoud assumes that Israel is following a tragic line. Israel cannot continue its occupation policies forever. She is correct that Hamas lacks the ability to build a viable Gaza. Still it remains that, politically speaking – in reality rather than in global public opinion – Israel is doing quite well. Israel's invasion of the West Bank and bombing of Gaza has further strengthened its stranglehold on Palestine.

Hamas is a failure. I agree. But with Israel and Egypt's control of Gaza's borders no government could succeed.

So, too, the Palestinian Authority. As big a failure. But with Israel's occupation no government could succeed.

The ceasefire? What it offers Gaza is the status quo – with a little more food and materials, some operating tunnels, restricted access to Egypt and a few other items that keeps everything that was in place. Minus the recent and accumulating destruction meted out.

That is, if the ceasefire is implemented. If it holds.

A ceasefire doesn't change the designed-to-fail Palestinian governing bodies. Or the designed-to-fail Palestinian society. Or Israel's dominance.

Untangling the (un)Holy Land is difficult. Too many moving and immovable parts. Nonetheless, the political task remains. Settling for a ceasefire is to admit failure and create the context for further failure.

A ceasefire tightens rather than untangles the Gordian Knot of occupation and destruction.

Is this what Israel, the United States, Europe and the Arab world really want?

The Palestinian people deserve an answer rather than a ceasefire that promises failure and destruction without end.

Aaron & Isaiah
Jews of Conscience

I AM A JEW.
ISRAEL IS NOT MY STATE.

Ceasefires come and go. Until there is one that stays, then comes and goes again.

Public statements, accusations and moral outcries proliferate. Old voices are heard from again. New voices join the fray.

The Israeli and Palestinian political broadsides are the worse. Posturing and more posturing. Hypocrisy of the highest order.

Even B'Tselem, normally on the straight and narrow, panders to the Israeli public. Why else release such a ridiculous report that characterizes the weapons fired from Gaza as action that "defies humanity and is morally and legally reprehensible."

Resistance is resistance. It isn't pretty. But then neither is oppression.

Not to leave out the new fascist dictatorship in Egypt and its ceasefire remedy. The great negotiator of peace and democracy for the ages! I can't stomach reading their communiques. Even for the jaded, they're just too much.

Egypt should start at home. Negotiate a ceasefire in its war against the Muslim Brotherhood, journalists and dissenters, then think about the Palestinians that, like Israel, it is oppressing.

John Kerry is back on the scene. Is he the statements he makes, the documents he releases or is he an apparition that periodically appears in different parts of the world?

When Kerry threatened to appear in Cairo to broker a ceasefire, the Egyptian dictator told him to stay home. Dictator Abdel Fattah el-Sisi and Prime Minister for Life, Benjamin Netanyahu, would work it out themselves. With the corrupt Tony Blair it appears. Which they did. Sort of.

Finally, church pleas for peace. It seems that the churches love everyone, Jews, Christians and Muslims, thus their pleas for peace. As if historically Christians have been on the side of the angels.

Christwashing. Unfortunately, the churches newly-found inclusive love hides the sins of the churches today.

These announcements are like knocks on the door – or knock on roof missile warnings in our up-to-date Israeli parlance. Once they're heard it's already too late.

The real casualties continue to mount in an almost comical ratio. As I write it is two hundred or so Palestinians dead to one Israeli. The ratio of injured is even more lopsided, if that is statistically possible.

As for my own children, the die has been cast. A few days ago, my little one, Isaiah, soon to be a senior in college, posted this on Facebook:

> I am a Jew (period)
> Israel is NOT my state (period)
> Judaism does not equal Israel (period)

Definitive and cogent. Too easy? Mind you, this was before the four children were killed on the Gaza beach yesterday.

Perhaps Isaiah lacks the sophistication of those Jewish pundits who trot out time-worn tropes like anti-Semitism, Hamas targeting civilians and the two rights / two wrongs theory as death once again reigns down on a defenseless civilian population. Or maybe Isaiah has heard all that, seen through it and says what's on his mind.

Isaiah is a Jew of Conscience – without "buts."

My big one, Aaron, is like that, too. On a trip to the (un)Holy Land, Aaron was involved in a demonstration against home demolitions. To his surprise, one of the Israeli soldiers told him that he respected and even agreed with his protest. When I tried to show Aaron how that attested to the possibility of change in the future, he replied: "Dad, what he said and then did – I lost my faith in humanity."

Like Isaiah, definitive and cogent. Too easy?

On the Jewish establishment's scale both Isaiah and Aaron are lost to Israel, and they are lost to the Jewish people.

Lost – or found?

If lost, what does that mean in relation to Israel's relentless military machine?

If found, what does that mean to the relentless militarization of Jewish life?

Israel will continue on its path regardless. And this will be how Jews are known throughout the world.

The Jewish witness in the future? We have already joined the vaunted realm of politics and the church. Posturing and more posturing. Hypocrisy of the highest order.

Is the Jewish witness beside the point, worrying too much about "us" and not enough about what's happening to Palestinians? Could be.

Still, imagine this even now – a world without Jews of Conscience. Would the world be better off having lost a primal root of dissent and relentless justice-seeking?

Israel is on the move, invading the West Bank, destroying homes, bombing Gaza, murdering children playing on the beach, kidnapping and burning Palestinians alive. But Israel is doing more than murdering Palestinians. Israel is trying to eliminate the very conscience that calls it to account.

Taking Aim
Al Azza Refugee Camp

ISRAEL'S IRON FIST

From Iron Dome to Iron Fist. This is how Naftali Bennett, Israel's economy minister, defined Israel's invasion of Gaza yesterday. Truth be known it was Iron Fist all along.

The difference between slow and quick death is important but death to the individual – and the collective – is defining. Israel has been killing Palestinians and Palestine since its inception. Israel's original sin of ethnic cleansing in peace and war continues.

Contra Christian doctrine, there's no way back from death. Life is what we have. With all the anxieties and difficulties involved, life beats the alternative. But where is life, or the opening to life, in Israel's Iron Fist?

In the West, we ask where the politicians and the churches are. Fair question. A statement on the crisis issued by the United Church of Christ is a beginning. Though there are questionable equations of power and responsibility, the statement ends with an important recommendation:

> *Take action to end the violence – for today, and for the future. Let your senators and representative know that as a person of faith, respecting the dignity of every human being you call on them to:*
>
> *Demand an immediate ceasefire by all parties.*
>
> *Condemn all violence against civilians, both by Palestinians and by Israeli forces. It is clear that rockets from Gaza target civilian areas in Israel. In Gaza, civilians are often in harm's way from Israeli fire, regardless of the intended target.*
>
> *Insist on an end to the Israeli occupation of Palestinian land, including full dismantlement of the barrier built on Palestinian land, and an end to the Gaza blockade.*

Recognize that U.S. diplomatic and financial support enable the occupation. The U.S. provides over $3 billion per year in military aid to Israel.

Condition military aid to Israel on its compliance with U.S. law and policy.

Strange to think politicians and churches without thinking about statements from mainstream Jewish organizations. Or have we long ago given up on any organized Jewish body speaking Jewish truth to Jewish power?

As of this writing J Street has yet to issue a statement beyond the one it issued on July 11th. Judging on this, expectations should be kept low when finally J Street finds their voice.

As per J Street, the July 11th statement contains an argument for both sides – the aspirations of Jews and Palestinians, their suffering etc. It is, more or less, balanced if skewing Israel with some concessions for Israel's wrong doing is so defined. But the problem remains. J Street still doesn't get the fact of the matter – Israel isn't stopping and won't abide a real Palestinian state. That's the beginning of the road back to reality, a road J Street will never take.

When will a Jewish mainstream statement contain, for example, the last two points made by the UCC? After all, if US foreign policy has carrots and sticks, in the Middle East, the US will be taken seriously only if aid and compliance with US law and policy are enforced.

Of course, if the US abided by its own righteous declarations, it might be easier to demand others do so too.

Evading the issue of Israel's foundation is critical. It is becoming more and more obvious. But no one on the moral ground of the West wants to go back to history – to 1948. Or thereafter. Or now. There are some who want Israel's "autonomy" solution. Others want another way. But the fundamental agreement for Palestinians is a restricted autonomy that appears to be a state.

This latest invasion of Gaza is less about genocide, contra Ilan Pappe, though his points, as always, are well taken. Rather, the point of Israel's invasion – like its continuing actions in the West Bank under Gaza's cover – is to finalize what most of the world, including the Arab world, really wants. What the world wants is a policy that contains Palestinians and leaves the Middle East order, at least what's left of it, in place.

If the policy of containment should be called genocide, so be it, but politically the strategy is a policy of managing a collective. Terminology like this might seem harsh. It is.

In the boardrooms of governing powers it sounds quite reasonable. And doable. That Palestinians have to give up their right to freedom is considered, if at all, collateral damage.

Is that what Palestinians in the West Bank and Gaza are experiencing? Are they indeed defined as part of the superfluous people of the world Hannah Arendt wrote about so many years ago, even as she wrote about Israel's destiny as a modern-day Sparta?

Superfluous populations. They're all over the world – as defined by the powers that be.

Gazans are dying by the hundreds. Soon it may be more. The moral outrage heard around the world is the outrage of those who cry out that there are no superfluous people anywhere, especially in Gaza.

John Kerry
US Secretary of State

The Other Side
of History

Iron death. What else is an iron fist engaged in war?

If it wasn't already, the massacre in Shuja'iyeh makes it abundantly clear. So the world's leaders are scrambling. US Secretary of State John Kerry is in Cairo hawking President Obama's call for an immediate ceasefire. Look for a Kerry Plan to emerge, even if it's never announced, as was the case with his vaunted end-it-all scheme that collapsed months ago.

From the Sunday talk programs and Kerry's unscripted sarcastic remark about Israel's "pinpoint" targeting of Hamas "terror" targets, we know Kerry knows. Remember his comment some months ago about Israeli apartheid? That was when his peace efforts were falling apart.

What is to be thought of world leaders who know the score in private and continually lie in public? They are little better than the Israelis gathered on the border of Gaza who cheer each Israeli bomb strike.

Maybe those Israeli bomb cheerleaders are not far off. Israel was born through violence. Israel has expanded through violence. Israel makes sure that there won't be a Palestinian state through violence.

Violence has become central to Jewish existence – in Israel and outside of it. Our violence is defining us as a people.

The announcement that an Israeli firm, Elbit Systems, will provide the surveillance system for the border fence between the US and Mexico is part and parcel of this violence. After all, Israel is an expert in border "control." Israel has the experience and technology to prove it. Why shouldn't Israel, the US, Europe and everyone else, take advantage of Israel's expertise in developing advanced apartheid technology?

Somewhat like Israel's arm industry and their experience in testing weapons against Palestinians. Who in the world rejects those Palestinian-tested armaments? Many who buy these weapons are now calling on Israel to halt the slaughter. Nation-State Hypocrisy 101.

Eyewitness accounts in Gaza say it all. If you're still on the fence about Israel's right to defend itself take a listen to Mads Gilbert. Unlike the diplomats, the doctors in Gaza know the human score.

Israel's gloves are off. There is less and less moral grandstanding.

Does the world's condemnation make Israel the ultimate loser in this latest Gaza war? I doubt it. If you remember, the 2008 Gaza war was thought to be the end of Israel's ability to violate international law. The world would never let Israel's aggression go unpunished again.

Like Israel's last invasion of Gaza, this invasion – with the parallel invasion of the West Bank – will work in Israel's favor. The soon to come ceasefire will leave the power equation intact, only more in Israel's favor. The US will seek Palestinian Authority control of Gaza as an obvious ploy for a severely truncated Palestinian autonomy in what is left of Palestine.

What's sad is that most of the world will back this plan as a way out for Palestinians.

So it goes in the world of power politics. After this long and arduous history, Jews and the state of Israel have learned, indeed refined, the political art of conquest as a way of life. Unlearning this art is essential but that is another long haul. More and more Jews won't think the hard work is worth it.

Palestinians are on the other side of history – as Jews once were. But, unlike Jews, their way back will be even more difficult. Like his predecessors, Prime Minister Netanyahu is determined to make the resurrection of Palestine impossible. Count Israel's Gaza invasion as part of that endgame.

Rabbi Irving Greenberg
United States

BURNING CHILDREN

Last night, during the murderous Israeli assault on Gaza, I heard from a friend who recalled a passage I wrote in 1987:

> *As risky and problematic as it is, we are called today to the wilderness; but the call is a promise of liberation. Chastened by history, we can no longer see liberation as the omnipotent preserve of God hovering over us by day and leading us by night, or simply as the search for the empowerment of our own people in America and Israel. We can ill afford such innocence in the presence of burning children, whether they be in Poland or in Palestine.*

Though hardly a neophyte to Israel's transgressions, my friend seemed shaken by the death toll in Gaza, the targeting of civilians, children being blown to bits. He was also reflecting on a *Wall Street Journal* Op-Ed by Thane Rosenbaum that views Israel's civilian massacres almost as a rite of passage. Jews and others should wake up to the violence, not of Israel, but of Hamas. Targeting civilians isn't as bad as it initially sounds. In fact, civilian deaths are inevitable. Get over it.

This is how Rosenbaum parses it:

> *The asymmetry is complicated even further by the status of these civilians. Under such maddening circumstances, are the adults, in a legal and moral sense, actual civilians? To qualify as a civilian one has to do more than simply look the part. How you came to find yourself in such a vulnerable state matters.*
>
> *After all, when everyone is wearing casual street clothing, civilian status is shared widely.*
>
> *The people of Gaza overwhelmingly elected Hamas, a terrorist outfit dedicated to the destruction of Israel, as their designated*

representatives. Almost instantly Hamas began stockpiling weapons and using them against a more powerful foe with a solid track record of retaliation.

What did Gazans think was going to happen? Surely they must have understood on election night that their lives would now be suspended in a state of utter chaos. Life expectancy would be miserably low; children would be without a future. Staying alive would be a challenge, if staying alive even mattered anymore.

Thus, the government in power – anywhere – defines the people's, including children's, right to life? Does this same reasoning apply for Palestinians in relation to Israel and Israeli children? Does electing and reelecting Netanyahu mean forfeiting their right to life?

Rosenbaum's logic is twisted. If enablers have their place at The Hague, such incitement will surely have its day in court.

The passage I wrote about burning children reflected the language of Rabbi Irving Greenberg, a prominent Holocaust theologian. It came to mind most vividly several weeks ago when Mohamed Abu Khdeir was burned alive after being kidnapped by several Israelis. The inversion of Jewish history was glaring. But I wondered if invoking the Holocaust made sense here. Would it be seen as dwelling in the past?

It was in a 1974 essay that Rabbi Greenberg first wrote about the burning children of the Holocaust as a challenge for the Jewish future. I have quoted this passage often:

After the Holocaust, no statement, theological or otherwise, should be made that would not be credible in the presence of the burning children.

Rabbi Greenberg's invocation of burning children came to life in a different way for me when I visited Palestinian hospitals during the first Palestinian Uprising in 1988 and 1989. There I saw Palestinians of all ages but mostly teenagers who had been shot by Israel's "rubber" bullets. Some were struggling for life. Others were already brain dead. I visited with the parents and siblings of the injured. Above the beds were martyr photos of the children framed by kefiyas.

After I left the hospitals, I wrote a poem about my experience. I used Rabbi Greenberg's haunting words about burning children to express my experience in the hospitals. In the poem I asked if these Palestinian children weren't, like the children of the Holocaust, burning too. I felt the Palestinian children I saw were in many ways "our" children. We share a common humanity as starters but for Jews I knew that their "burning" was our responsibility.

Though unintended by Rabbi Greenberg, his Holocaust statement has broadened to include Palestinians who are "burning," this time at the hands of Jews. What theological statement can we make about God that makes sense to the burning children of the Holocaust – and Palestine?

Speak about God – if it makes sense to the burning children of the Holocaust and Palestine. Taken seriously, the seminaries of every faith would have to close. As would the synagogues, churches and mosques. God-talk cannot make sense to a burning child.

Yet the most intriguing and difficult part of Rabbi Greenberg's words may be his clause – "or otherwise." Otherwise would include political, economic, ecological and military statements – and the policies that go with them.

Propose and implement these policies without question – if they make sense to the burning children.

Does Israel's invasion of Gaza pass this Holocaust test?

Does Israel's occupation of Palestine pass this Holocaust test?

Perhaps no war can pass Rabbi Greenberg's haunting thoughts. Should we then disband every army and shut down the arms producers worldwide, including in Israel?

Burning Children
A JEWISH VIEW OF THE WAR IN GAZA

As the news reports show and Palestinians know by experience, burning children have become a way of life for Israel. It makes sense to Israel's government and Jews around the world that supports the invasion of Gaza and even Op-Ed writers in the *Wall Street Journal*. The burning children of Gaza are collateral damage to a larger more important story.

Like Jewish children were considered not so long ago?

The children of Palestine tell another story – for themselves, for Jews and for history.

Chastened by history, indeed, Jews are by the Holocaust and now by Palestine.

For in Gaza right now children are burning everywhere.

Ready and Watiting
US Troops

ISRAEL'S DEFEAT

John Kerry in Israel. Is he preparing to offer US troops to help enforce a ceasefire in Gaza?

I wouldn't be surprised, though accepting an overt American military presence in or near Israel would be a first. Since Israel is an American military client state they might as well go all the way. It can only help Israel and, at least for the moment, the Palestinian Authority. Finishing off Hamas isn't Israel's plan anyway. Extending the PA's power is.

The world is abuzz with moral indignation and Israel's own losses continue to increase. But the ratio of Israeli and Palestinian deaths, not to mention those injured, is enormous and typical. Israeli deaths are well within what Israel's military expected. Like the civilians of Gaza, these soldiers are considered by Israel to be collateral damage.

Some pundits are calling Israel's invasion of Gaza a defeat. Even Israel's international airport is under assault and some airlines are refusing to land there. A blow to Israel's pride for sure. However, this analysis rests on the assumption that Israel goes to war to win – as in defeat the enemy once and for all. This assumption is false. No Israeli military analyst thinks Israel will win the Gaza war in the traditional sense of that term.

Rather Israel goes to war to buy time, to further de-develop Palestinian society and to go about its business elsewhere, say in the West Bank.

As for the ceasefire proposal by Hamas, it's a ten year humdinger that doesn't include real independence or even an end to occupation. Israel should accept this proposal as a gift.

If Gaza is quiet, imagine what the West Bank will look like in ten years.

So it goes. Of course, the people of Gaza need a ceasefire and a loosening of the noose. They need relief. In the next days expect a move from Iron Death back to the norm, Iron Fist.

The world will gladly oblige Gaza this. Don't expect much more.

In this time of outrage, it is important to think about what the world powers – including the United Nations – want and can deliver. Their desperate attempt to halt the bloodshed is noble. Yet sometimes the best laid plans are, in the long run, traps of unexpected dimensions.

Heading for the Gaza Strip
The War Torah

FABRICATED
MARTYRDOM ?

The Holy Land is a strange place to live and to worship. Anyone who has studied the history of the Holy Land or lived there knows its twists and turns of politics and faith are the stuff of legend. Which is part of the problem.

Just the monotheistic religions are enough to insure the Holy Land's importance and conflictive contribution to the world's landscape. Is there another city like Jerusalem, one that has contributed so much justice, love and violence to our global patrimony?

The Holy Land is a gift that keeps on giving. Like an endowment of sorts, the interest on the principle is more than lose change.

Like the notion of a Palestinian state that doesn't resemble any state in existence.

Or the on and off ceasefire in the Gaza war. It seems that Israel wants the ability to keep its military working overtime destroying tunnels and other aspects of Palestinian life while the Palestinians lay down their arms and promise quiet on Israel's border.

Like the Palestinian state, this ceasefire doesn't resemble any that I know of.

Now word is that the Israeli soldier captured in Gaza might have been killed – with his Palestinian captors – by the Israeli military. Evidently a principle in Israel's army is that no Jewish life is to be found among Palestinians, even a prisoner of war. The exceptions, at least for the time being, are settlers in Jerusalem and the West Bank.

This is how Richard Silverstein tells the story:

> I've devoted a good deal of my life to Israel. I've studied, read, visited, lived, breathed it. Not in the way diehard pro-Israel fanatics do. But in a different way that matched my own intellectual and political proclivities. It's a subject that is rich, varied, troubling, bedeviling, and exhilarating. But every once in a while I learn something I never thought possible; and I don't mean this in a good way.
>
> Tonight, my Israeli source informed me that Sgt. Guy Levy, serving in the armored corps, was captured by Hamas fighters. He had been part of a joint engineering-armored-combat unit searching for tunnels. Troops entered a structure and discovered a tunnel. Suddenly, out of the shaft sprang two militants who dragged one of the soldiers into it. By return fire, one of the Palestinians was killed, while the other fled, presumably with the soldier.
>
> This Israeli report, which was censored by the IDF, says only that the attempt to capture the soldier failed. It says nothing about his fate. The expectation of anyone reading it would be that the soldier was freed. But he was not. In order to prevent the success of the operation, the IDF killed him. Nana reports that the IDF fired a tank shell into the building, which is the same way another captured soldier was killed by the IDF during Cast Lead.

I can't verify this report, though it certainly rings true. Individual sacrifice for the collective, like the history of the Holy Land, has its own interesting history. Jews are raised with a history of martyrdom. Palestinians are experiencing martyrdom en masse today. But martyrdom for the Jewish state? If it is indeed martyrdom. Or is Levy's death – along with other Israeli military deaths – sacrifice for a certain political sensibility within Israel?

Some would say that Israeli soldiers who die for the Jewish state are martyrs on behalf of the Jewish people. With so many Jews of Conscience testifying against such a notion, it is difficult to raise these deaths to that level.

Indeed, Jews of Conscience are trying to save Palestinians – and Jews – from such a fate.

Are these Israeli deaths in vain? Even after the various ceasefires, Gaza will remain. Palestinian resistance isn't going away.

Is their martyrdom fabricated? Like the Israeli invasion of the West Bank trying to "save" the kidnapped teenagers was fabricated? The government knew the teens were dead. The government also knows how many Israelis will die in Gaza.

Martyrs that aren't martyrs. This, too, has a long history.

Even the question of who "our" martyrs are is becoming more and more difficult to discern. Are the Israeli soldiers who die "our" martyrs? Or, in one of the great reversals in Jewish history, are the Palestinian martyrs somehow, also, "our" own?

Amira Hass
West Bank

AMIRA HASS
AND THE END OF JEWISH ETHICAL HISTORY

I like and admire Amira Hass. Her reporting is admirable and more. As a daughter of Holocaust survivors, she has lived through and commented on the contemporary arc of Jewish history. From the Holocaust to the devastating violence of Israel's occupation mark her reporting, along with Gideon Levy and others, as the epitome of Jewish conscience. Hass is giving her all at the end of Jewish ethical history.

In her recent writing on Gaza, Hass's words are strong and moving. They are also increasingly disconnected. As I once did and perhaps still do, Hass lives in a Jewish ethical history that no longer exists. Rather than addressing current events, her words represent mourning for a world that will not be resurrected.

Hass's particular mistake is clear. Contra her analysis, Israel's invasion of Gaza isn't hurting Israel. Rather, it's paving the way for the future that most Israelis – and Jews – actually want and embrace. That future is low on ethics and high on power. As everywhere in the world.

Here are some of Hass's moving words:

> If victory is measured by the success at causing lifelong trauma to 1.8 million people (and not for the first time) waiting to be executed any moment–then the victory is yours.

> These victories add up to our moral implosion, the ethical defeat of a society that now engages in no self-inspection, that wallows in self-pity over postponed airline flights and burnishes itself with the pride of the enlightened. This is a society that mourns, naturally, its more than 40 soldiers who were killed, but at the same time hardens its heart and mind in the face of all the suffering and moral courage and heroism of the

people we are attacking. A society that does not understand the extent to which the balance of forces is against it.

"In all the suffering and death," wrote a friend from Gaza, "there are so many expressions of tenderness and kindness. People are taking care of one another, comforting one another. Especially children who are searching for the best way to support their parents. I saw many children no older than 10 years old who are hugging, comforting their younger siblings, trying to distract them from the horror. So young and already the caretakers of someone else. I did not meet a single child who did not lose someone – a parent, grandmother, friend, aunt or neighbor. And I thought: If Hamas grew out of the generation of the first intifada, when the young people who threw stones were met with bullets, who will grow out of the generation that experienced the repeated massacres of the last seven years?"

Our moral defeat will haunt us for many years to come.

States don't live on morality – even a Jewish state. If the state has enough power, a moral haunting may be experienced by a minority. Jews of Conscience in Israel and beyond are examples of this. But the majority of any state's citizens want to get on with their lives and enjoy the benefits accrued through military victory and economic imperialism.

The very powers so concerned with Gaza attest to this lack of moral haunting. Whatever moral clauses invoked against Israeli power and on behalf of suffering Palestinians, where would Europe and America be without historical and contemporary empire?

What Hass wants is a return to a Jewish world and history that formed her. Though she knows this world was tainted, she still hopes that somehow the overall thrust of Jewish ethical history can pull us through. Hass is wrong. However one defines the Jewish condition, Jews like Hass continue to argue for a Jewish morality in the state of Israel that no longer exists.

Hass isn't a religious Jews, even a closeted one as far as I know. But her sense of the Jewish ethical and the punishment for Jewish wrongdoing, even in an imagined Palestinian resistance that knows no bounds, is a kind of faith. As a Jew, Hass can't give up on it. What Jewish and Israeli legs would she have to stand on if she threw in the ethical towel and admitted to her readers – and most of all to herself – that Jews and Jewish life have reached its end point?

Israel won't be haunted by its transgressions. When the end of the Israeli-Palestinians disputations finally arrives all will be forgiven on the international front.

Moral outrage by the powers of the world is limited by their own moral transgressions. They, too, have been forgiven rather than haunted by their power.

Should Israel be any different in reality than in the Jewish imagination?

Leonardo Boff
Brazil

LIBERATION THEOLOGY
AND THE WAR IN GAZA

To many, Leonardo Boff is a prophet. As a Brazilian Roman Catholic liberation theologian for many years, Boff is respected on the religious left for his outspoken critique of injustice within and outside of the church. His influence is so wide and his ideas so radical that some years ago he was censored by the Vatican in Rome.

In a wide-ranging interview in *Iglesia Descalza*, Boff spoke about the new Pope with ease and respect. His words and endorsement carry currency in Brazil and beyond:

> *Times have changed and thank God we have a Pope who, for the first time in 500 years, responds to reform, responds to Luther. Luther launched what we call the Protestant Principle, which is the principle of freedom. And this Pope lives it. And he doesn't see Christianity as a bunch of truths that you adhere to, but as the living encounter with Jesus. He distinguishes between Jesus' tradition—that set of ideals and traditions—and the Christian religion, which is equal to any other religion. He says: "I belong to the Jesus movement", and not to the Catholic religion. Such statements are outrageous to traditional Christians, but are absolutely correct in the theological sense—what we always said and were persecuted for.*

> *And I'm glad that the Church is no longer a body that embarrasses us, but a body that could help humanity make the difficult crossing to a different kind of society that respects the rights of nature, of the Earth, concerned about the future of life. I myself have been in touch with the Pope and his central theme is life. Human life, that of the earth, of nature. And we have to save it, because we have all the tools to destroy it.*

Though Boff's words on the Pope, especially his opening to gays and abortion, are important and in Catholic circles controversial, no doubt his reflections on Gaza – and Jews – will also garner attention. Though short, they are worthy of further reflection:

> *This pope is absolutely contemporary and necessary. I think he's the only world leader who is listened to and eventually could mediate this war of criminal massacre that Israel is carrying out against Gaza.*
>
> *And I think much of the blame rests with Obama, who is a criminal. Because no drone (unmanned aircraft) attack could be done without his personal license. They are using all sorts of weapons of destruction. They've closed Gaza complete, it has been turned into a concentration camp, and they will destroy it. So you have a country that was the victim of Nazism and uses Nazi methods to create victims. This is the great contradiction.*
>
> *And the United States supports them—Obama and all the presidents are victims of the great Jewish lobby that has two branches: the branch of the big banks and the media branch. They have enormous power over the presidents who don't want to alienate them and follow whatever these radical extremist Jews united with the Christian religious Right say. This is combined with a president like Obama who hasn't the least bit of humanitarian feeling, the compassion to say "stop the slaughter."*

Boff places the blame for Gaza on several levels. Israel is the most obvious to blame, so much so that it is largely unstated. Instead, Boff singles out Barack Obama for blame and circles back toward Israel and Jews – those who were victims of Nazis are now using Nazi methods to create the victims of Gaza. Boff notes the "great contradiction" without explanation. This, too, is obvious.

Then Boff becomes more specific. He links Gaza, Israel and Obama with the "great Jewish lobby," the branches of which consist of the banks and the media. Boff characterizes the Jewish lobby as consisting of "radical extremist Jews" who, notably, are united with the Christian religious right. So if Boff is seen as promoting a conspiratorial sense of history – which no doubt he will be – Jews are present, along with Christians. Obama and perhaps by extension the United States is located at the center.

With the surge of feeling about Israel and Jews surrounding the Gaza war and Israeli policy toward Palestinians in general, what are we to make of Boff's brief comments? This is important especially because the Jewish establishment has consistently tried to taint liberation theology with the broad brush of anti-Semitism.

This is the case even though liberation theology has for the most part steered clear of the Israel-Palestine issue.

For many years, the Jewish establishment has focused on liberation theology's use of Jesus as the liberator of the poor. Perhaps subconsciously the Jewish establishment knew that liberation theology's commitment to the poor of the world would inevitably involve a critique of Jewish power in Israel and beyond.

Will Boff's calling out of the Jewish lobby and radical extremist Jews be relegated to the stereotypes of Jewish control of the global economy and media? Or will those who are interested in the suffering of the Palestinian people place themselves in solidarity with Jews of Conscience who are battling the same forces Boff calls out in a language that needs a deeper encounter?

After all, like most peoples, including the citizens of Brazil – and as Boff knows well from his own experience with the Catholic Church – Jews exist on both sides of the empire divide. For every Jewish lobbyist there is a Jew of Conscience – and sometimes more.

Amos Oz
Jerusalem

Amos Oz
on Gaza

Here we go again. Ceasefires that don't hold. The excuse this time: an Israeli soldier has fallen into Palestinian hands. At least that's the word from Israel and the US State Department.

Ceasefires that don't hold are less about an Israeli soldier than they are about outside powers like the United States that are so concerned about Palestinian suffering that they transfer weapons to keep Israel's army on the move.

Ceasefires that don't hold are about strategic advantage, gas and oil fields and corporate profit.

For Palestinians, ceasefires that don't hold are about more burning children.

Ceasefires that don't hold are also about a people on the other side of history being bombed into oblivion by those who earnestly built the United States Holocaust Memorial Museum and solemnly pledge that never again should the world stand by in silence while Jews or anyone else suffers injustice and genocide.

Perhaps that pledge has been fulfilled in a strange and inverted way. The world is decidedly vocal about the injustice and violence Israel is visiting upon Palestinians. Even parts of the mainstream media are broadcasting the reality in part or in whole. Yet the world remains unwilling or unable to stop the carnage.

Thus Jeffrey Goldberg's fear that the capture of the Israeli soldier might cause Israeli military policy to go "all-in," or as the title of his commentary puts it, go "off the rails."

What could going off the rails mean in this situation? Israel is ravaging entire cities, rocketing hospitals, shelling UN schools and shelters. What's left in Netanyahu's "all-in" strategy – the overt ethnic cleansing of Gaza? The nuclear option?

Goldberg features Amos Oz, that venerable and much-feted Israeli novelist, peacenik and enabler of denigration of Palestinians, as Israel's "all-in" weather vane. If Oz becomes convinced that more violence is needed then Israel might indeed go off the rails.

If Oz is the person with his finger in the dam of Israeli rage, then all-in could become a reality in a heartbeat. Here is Oz in the interview itself:

> **Would you consider the present ground offensive to be limited or unlimited?**
>
> *I think in some points it is excessive. I don't have detailed information on what is actually happening on the ground, but to judge from some of the hits that the Israeli army caused in Gaza, I think at least in some points the military action is excessive–justified, but excessive.*
>
> **Can you imagine a Palestinian state that is not hostile toward Israel?**
>
> *Absolutely. I believe the majority of the Palestinians are not in love with Israel, but they do accept with clenched teeth that the Israeli Jews are not going anywhere, just like the majority of Israeli Jews–unhappily and with clenched teeth–accept that the Palestinians are here to stay. This is a basis not for a honeymoon, but perhaps for a fair divorce just like the case of the Czech Republic and Slovakia.*
>
> **You have been talking about a long-term solution. But what could a short-term agreement look like?**
>
> *The present hostilities will only stop, unfortunately, when one of the parties or both of them are exhausted. This morning*

I read very carefully the charter of Hamas. It says that the Prophet commands every Muslim to kill every Jew everywhere in the world. It quotes the Protocols of the Elders of Zion and says that the Jews controlled the world through the League of Nations and through the United Nations, that the Jews caused the two world wars and that the entire world is controlled by Jewish money. So I hardly see a prospect for a compromise between Israel and Hamas. I have been a man of compromise all my life. But even a man of compromise cannot approach Hamas and say: 'Maybe we meet halfway and Israel only exists on Mondays, Wednesdays and Fridays.'

Oz hasn't hopped off his highly-honored fence yet but, if you read his words carefully, don't tempt him. If Palestinians get too uppity, he might join the raging crowd.

As usual, though, the question is what is tolerated by the world that counts, the ones that tally the global scorecard. Israel's level of violence has until now been defined as "on the rails." Can we expect the world to refuse to tolerate another level of violence it defines as "off the rails?" Or will an "all-in" Israel continue to be tolerated and enabled?

Amos Oz wants the world to know that he is busy carefully reading Hamas's charter. But perhaps the world needs to read Amos Oz carefully.

Literary giant or not, Oz is ready to pull the plug. Can Israel be far behind?

Benjamin Netanyahu
Prime Minister of Israel

THE WITHDRAWAL
THAT ISN'T

Whether it is done, mostly done or just waiting for another opportunity to strike hard, Israel's announced "withdrawal" from Gaza is a brilliant move. In one stroke, Israel at least partially removes its soldiers from the battlefield, maintains its ability to bomb from the air and sea and defies the most public aspects of international mediating efforts.

Yesterday that is exactly what happened. More bombing. More carnage. More death.

Israel's Prime Minister Benjamin Netanyahu isn't keeping his cards close to the vest. Ever the bully, Netanyahu promises Hamas that it will pay an "intolerable price" if it continues firing rockets into Israel. Meanwhile, Israel's military will "prepare for continuing action according to our security needs and only according to our security needs."

So Israel is buying time, accomplishing what it wants, even as it thumbs its nose at the international community.

In its mind at least, no one in the world – not even the United States – tells Israel what it can and can't do. The most amazing aspect of Israel's strategy is that it works. No matter world opinion, Israel accomplishes its goal of further setting Gaza and the entire Palestinian enterprise back for years.

If the fighting eventually dies down, over the next weeks the rebuilding of Gaza will begin. Gaza's partners will return. A new incarnation of the Goldstone Report will take shape. Israel will also thumb its nose at both. Gaza will remain an open air prison.

Meanwhile the burning children – and adults – of Gaza will be left to their own devices. The posturing of the outraged global community will make little difference in their prospects for the future. Likely, Hamas will stay in place or some variation thereof. Perhaps a unity government will be (re) announced. Egypt will work closely with Israel and the Palestinian Authority to quiet Gaza. Disguised as statehood, autonomy talks will reappear.

If luck holds, John Kerry will fade from the newspapers for a while. His posturing as a lone courageous figure seeking first a lasting peace then negotiating a ceasefire – both of which failed miserably – will be consigned to the dustbin of history where hypocritical political figures' double talk defines them.

What are the lessons of Gaza for the NGOs, religious communities and people of conscience on the ground and around the world?

As the burning children of Gaza are accounted for, there needs to be a reckoning. It won't come from the powers that be. Will it come from the institutions that have expressed such moral outrage at Israel's behavior?

Such a reckoning won't matter – it won't be authentic – unless the institutions that serve the Palestinian people note their own failures.

Despite their best intentions, these institutions are invested in the status quo. They are in many ways enablers of Israeli power.

Moral outrage has run its course. It simply isn't enough.

Of course, as the day turns the siege of Gaza might intensify again. As if it could get worse.

Elie Wiesel
United States

ELIE WIESEL
PLAYS THE HOLOCAUST TRUMP CARD IN GAZA

Just when you thought it couldn't get worse, it does. I'm not thinking about the actual war in Gaza – that's bad enough.

It's the Jewish civil war over Israel, a civil war that includes both sides appealing to non-Jews and American foreign policy.

Of course, it's also about the Holocaust, that vast swathe of traumatized Jewish identity that keeps breaking open even as Israel's occupation regime and war machine go haywire.

The veterans of Holocaust discourse are older now, all in their eighties, but periodically they're trotted out to support Israel – especially when there isn't any viable way of doing so.

Call it the Holocaust trump card. Elie Wiesels wild.

Elie Wiesel can't help himself. If he hasn't debased himself and his cause enough on the subject of Israel in recent years, his latest is a stunner.

Teaming up with Shmuley Boteach, a rabbi whose book on Kosher sex made a splash some years ago and has been gaming right ever since, Wiesel has just penned a paid statement making the rounds of major newspapers and other media outlets.

Wiesel's theme? "Jews rejected child sacrifice 3,000 years ago. Now it's Hamas' turn."

The theme is a play on God's command to sacrifice Isaac. With Israel's invasion of Gaza, God's last minute decision to let Isaac live doesn't work at all.

The press release lays out Wiesel's campaign:

> *New York, NY August 1, 2014–In a stirring advertising campaign organized by Rabbi Shmuley's organization, This World: The Values Network, which seeks to disseminate universal Jewish values in politics, media, and culture as well as defend the State of Israel, Nobel Peace Laureate, Elie Wiesel, invokes the story of Abraham and the sacrifice of Isaac to frame the modern conflict between Israel and Hamas.*
>
> *Wiesel states that though Abraham lifts his knife to sacrifice his own son Isaac, his hand is stayed by God's own command, thereby rejecting child sacrifice forever. He added that, "Jews rejected child sacrifice 3500 years ago. Now it's Hamas' turn." Prof. Wiesel argues that while the suffering of those in Gaza is immense and a true tragedy, the blame lies solely with Hamas who use children as human shields and stores rockets and ammunitions in nurseries, schools, hospitals, and family homes.*

Wiesel's autobiographical classic, *Night*, has been read by millions. It's required reading for vast numbers of American school children. *Night's* new translation even received Oprah's seal of approval.

But the Jewish establishment doesn't seem to get it. Playing the Holocaust trump card isn't working anymore. Few respond to their Holocaust pleadings as they did almost reflexively decades ago.

Call if cognitive dissonance – using Jewish suffering as a rallying call while Jews cause suffering to others in the name of that suffering is too confusing for most folks. Say the Holocaust and people think Gaza. It isn't a comparison. It's a deep revulsion to violence in the name of innocents suffering.

The problem is the news that keeps coming from Israel. Israel's bombing of residential areas, hospitals and UN schools and shelters is international news. In Gaza, even after Israel's proclaimed "withdrawal," the death toll mounts. Among the dead are children sacrificed for Israel's obvious goal – to deny Palestinians statehood, their political and human rights, which include the right to resist occupation.

The question for Elie Wiesel and the Jewish establishment is not about Abraham's binding of Isaac – a treasure trove for interpreters of all types – but how many Palestinian children in Gaza will be sacrificed on the altar of Israel's national security.

If God stayed Abraham's knife, who will stay Israel's?

Hajar Muharram
Gaza

AFTER GAZA

Yet another ceasefire is in place. If it doesn't hold, more carnage will occur until another ceasefire is agreed to.

Israel's invasion can only go so far. With 1.8 million Gazans with nowhere to go, short of a mass expulsion – again there is nowhere else to go – as more than a few Israeli commentators have noted, Israel is stuck with Gaza. They don't seem to ask the obvious question: What kind of future does being "stuck" with Gaza portend for Israel let alone Palestinians?

Already the aftermath of Israel's invasion is being prepared for. A massive rebuilding effort will have to take place and life and death health emergencies proliferate. The injured need medicine. The dead need burial. Food and water? Electricity? Israel has decimated Gaza's infrastructure – sewage facilities, electric plants, hospitals – the very lifeblood of any society. Was this Israel's plan all along, to once again set Palestinian life back, to keep Gaza and the Palestinian people picking up their pieces so their long sought freedom would be permanently delayed?

Another preparation: Israel's day in court. Already a case against Israel for war crimes in Gaza is being prepared. The "Joint Declaration on International Law and Gaza" is strong, well-stated and heartbreaking. Its opening paragraphs tell the story:

> According to UN sources, over the last three weeks, at least 1,373 Palestinians in Gaza have been killed and 8,265, including 2,502 children and 1,626 women, have been injured. Several independent sources indicate that only 15 per cent of the casualties were combatants. Entire families have been murdered. Hospitals, clinics, as well as a rehabilitation centre for disabled persons have been targeted and severely damaged. During one single day, on Sunday 20th July, more

than 100 Palestinian civilians were killed in Shuga'iya, a residential neighbourhood of Gaza City. This was one of the bloodiest and most aggressive operations ever conducted by Israel in the Gaza Strip, a form of urban violence constituting a total disrespect of civilian innocence. Sadly, this was followed only a couple of days later by an equally destructive attack on Khuza'a, East of Khan Younis.

Additionally, the offensive has already caused widespread destruction of buildings and infrastructure: according to the UN Office for the Coordination of Humanitarian Affairs, over 3,300 houses have been targeted resulting in their destruction or severe damage.

As denounced by the UN Fact-Finding Mission (FFM) on the Gaza conflict in the aftermath of Israel's 'Operation Cast Lead' in 2008-2009: "While the Israeli Government has sought to portray its operations as essentially a response to rocket attacks in the exercise of its right to self defence, the Mission considers the plan to have been directed, at least in part, at a different target: The people of Gaza as a whole" (A/HRC/12/48, par. 1883). The same can be said for the current Israeli offensive.

International law is one important element in the aftermath of Israel's invasion of Gaza. But to leave aside a deeper reckoning of other actors – the United Nations, NGOs, churches – would be a mistake. From the Jewish perspective, Israel's criminality cuts even deeper to the bone. What are Jews of Conscience in and outside of Israel to make of the militarism that has taken hold in Jewish life? Is there a way back to some kind of sanity, respect for others and, as well, respect for ourselves?

If Israel is stuck with Gaza are Jews stuck with Israel?

Michael Lerner, a longtime Jewish dissident, wrote the following as the latest ceasefire was declared:

BURNING CHILDREN
A **JEWISH** VIEW OF THE WAR IN GAZA

My heart is broken as I witness the suffering of the Palestinian people and the seeming indifference of Israelis. Tonight (August 4) and tomorrow (August 5), which mark Tisha B'av, the Jewish commemoration of disasters that happened to us through Jewish history, I'm going to be fasting and mourning also for a Judaism being murdered by Israel. No matter who gets blamed for the breakdowns in the cease fire or for "starting" this latest iteration of a struggle that is at least 140 years old, one of the primary victims of the war between Israel and Hamas is the compassionate and love-oriented Judaism that has held together for several thousand years. Even as Israel withdraws its troops from Gaza, leaving behind immense devastation, over 1,800 dead Gazans, and over four thousand wounded, without adequate medical supplies because of Israel's continuing blockade, Israeli Prime Minister Netanyahu refuses to negotiate a cease fire, fearful that he would be seen as "weak" if Israel gave way to Gazans' demand for an end to the blockade and a freeing of thousands of Palestinian prisoners kidnapped and held in Israeli jails in violation of their human rights.

The title of Lerner's essay – "I'm a Rabbi in Mourning for a Judaism Being Murdered by Israel" – as with his words – is provocative. But Lerner raises more questions than he realizes. Is the issue for Jews primarily what Palestinian suffering means for Jews and, more specifically, for Judaism? Saving Israel, even saving Judaism, can't be the primary goal for Jews, can it? For even if Palestinians were miraculously freed after one of these ceasefires, Israel, Judaism and Jewish history would be permanently damaged. It's not about setting Palestinians free and then building a fence so that Jews inside and outside of Israel can go about our business as if nothing has happened. A return to Jewish innocence is hardly in the cards. Should it be hoped for?

Lerner's return to a Judaism of love and compassion is a mirage, itself an idyllic idol, a symbol of false consciousness that is the mirror image of Israel's violence. All religions and communities are complicated. Judaism is no different. In Judaism and Jewish life there is love and compassion.

There is also hate and violence. Lerner's vision of Judaism and Jewish life is authentic – partly. Israel's Prime Minister Benjamin Netanyahu vision of Jewish life is authentic – partly.

As with the divisions in Christianity and Islam, the question for every generation is which vision will win out. It is rare that a complete victory will be achieved. Rather, we are left with partial victories and often too many defeats. Thus Jewish mourning or, on the other side of coin, Jewish cheerleading needs to be tempered by the realities of the struggle ahead. Jewish Voice for Peace, an activist dissident organization, is trumpeting its growth and vitality that Israel's invasion of Gaza has occasioned. But, like Lerner, they should be chastened.

The statement by Rabbi Alissa Wise, Co-Director of Organizing and Chair of the Jewish Voice for Peace Rabbinical Council that – "Every time Israel engages in high-profile repression of civilians, we get inundated. But we have never seen anything like this. Our mailing list grew by 50,000 in 3 weeks and we can't keep up with the demand for new chapters. This is the final straw for many Jews, who have decided that their silence implies consent"– is encouraging but needs to be understood in a broader context.

Post-invasion, Israel is stronger than ever. Though global public opinion strongly resonates with the Palestinian cause, the Jewish part of that solidarity, though growing, remains small. And Israel, no matter its claim to exist and act on behalf of the Jewish people, is no longer dependent on Jewish opinion and support. Israel's claim as a Jewish state remains – as it charts its own destiny.

Writing of Elie Wiesel's statement on Hamas and child sacrifice, a claim belied by the evidence, I ended my reflection: "If Abraham's knife was stayed by God, who will stay Israel's knife?"

One proposal involving BDS and the one-state solution comes from Ilan Pappe, an Israeli academic in exile. Just before the ceasefire, Pappe was interviewed by *The White Review*. His responses cover a lot of ground including the possibility of a solution to the Israeli-Palestinian conflict:

Q: You are a supporter of the Boycott, Divestment and Sanctions (BDS) movement, which has been criticised by both Noam Chomsky and Norman Finklestein, among others, the latter going so far as to describe it as a 'cult'. What are your reasons for supporting it?

Pappe: *I wonder whether this is a question any more after the current Israeli atrocities in Gaza. Can Chomsky and Finklestein offer us an alternative strategy apart from repeating the overused mantra of the 'Two-State Solution'? This is the only way forward given Israeli brutality and the balance of power on the ground.*

Q: Could you specify your difficulties with the 'Two-State Solution'?

Pappe: *It is a solution for only a part of the Palestinians and for only a part of Palestine. The Palestinians in Israel (one in every five citizens in Israel is a Palestinian) and the refugees have been left out of this arrangement, and they constitute fifty per cent of the Palestinian people. The whole body is ill and we offer to treat only one hand. Secondly, the only Palestinian state Israel can agree to will have no sovereignty for the Palestinians and no territorial integrity. Finally, the Israelis have colonised the West Bank to such an extent that there is no way of finding a reasonable space for such a state.*

Q: On what grounds do you support a 'One State Solution'?

Pappe: *Firstly, because it is the only solution that will enable the Palestinian refugees of 1948 to return, which for me is a precondition for peace. Secondly, it will also bring an end to the Apartheid experienced by Palestinians inside Israel. And, finally, the facts established by Israel in the last forty-five years are far more important than those established in the first twenty years of the occupation. There is no room for a viable mini-state of Palestine and there is no reason to assume that such a state will end the conflict.*

Q: A United Nations report on the Gaza Strip has claimed that the area 'will not be liveable by 2020.' In your opinion, how long can the occupation go on?

Pappe: *I think in many ways we are at the beginning of a new Intifada. If it does not explode now, it will explode in a few years. So the occupation will not go on forever. The question is at what price and will the international community intervene to stop it.*

In Pappe's view after Gaza, the two-state solution is dead, BDS is on the rise and a one-state solution is the only way forward. In the meantime, a new Palestinian uprising is around the corner. In short, because these Palestinian uprisings almost always lead to Israeli invasions, Pappe envisions more of the same – until both sides realize that the thought and reality of a separation between Jews and Palestinians is ethically unjust and, on a practical level, untenable.

Pappe might be right. Obviously the two-state solution is dead. Palestinian resistance to occupation and ghettoization will continue. Jews and Palestinians living together in equality and peace is an obvious way forward. Nonetheless, everyone who knows the political scorecard in the Middle East, including Pappe, know that the one-state solution is a futuristic scenario that is decades or more away. My own sense is this living arrangement is even further away, if it will ever come to pass. The struggle of Jews and Palestinians is deeply particular rather than universal. From my vantage point, it isn't even clear that Palestinians would benefit from the integration Pappe seeks.

Here is where the progressive interpretation of Israel-Palestine departs from the utopian sensibilities that, at the same time, seem so practical, even obvious. Especially from the Jewish side, it is disingenuous to argue that Jews are universalists in general. Jews are peculiar universalists in that their universal arguments circle back to their Jewishness. Having said that, Palestinians who argue a universal sensibility, even those famed universalist Palestinians like the late Edward Said, are much more complicated then they appear or think themselves to be. Whether it's from a long history or their experience with displacement, occupation, exile and diaspora, Palestinians have a healthy sense of their own particularity. Jews have a strong sense of historic destiny. So do Palestinians.

Is there a way forward that honors Jewish and Palestinian particularity and broadens into – also – a shared destiny? After Gaza, a full two-state political reality seems to be the first step forward. That is nowhere to be seen. However, at no time in the history of Israel-Palestine have we been further from the one-state reality Pappe and others envision. The one-state we have is Israel controlling all of Palestine from Tel Aviv to the Jordan River. All negotiations, including the ones that are beginning anew now, accept that fact. Even the ten year truce that Hamas has offered Israel, assumes Israel's control of Palestine. Of course, such a truce with Gaza would have ramifications for Jerusalem and the West Bank. Knowing what Jerusalem and the West Bank look like today, with the hundreds of thousands Israeli settlers already in place along with the infrastructure this demands – what Jeff Halper calls the "matrix of control" – imagine what a Palestinian state would look like in a decade.

Thus the Palestinian Nakba, the catastrophe, will continue well beyond Gaza. Over the coming months a call for Israel to be tried for war crimes will gain momentum. It's likely as well that some form of the Kerry initiative will be reintroduced. But that formula, though never officially detailed, in its broad articulation only sought a finalized autonomy for Palestinians in the West Bank. Jerusalem and Gaza were hardly mentioned. The idea might be to extend the Palestinian Authority's presence into Gaza, eliminating Hamas and the elements that even Hamas cannot control. Yet that would only extend the range of limited autonomy. Israel – with the United States, Egypt and Jordan – would be calling the Palestinian shots. Few outside the rarefied atmosphere of empire control think that the Kerry initiative has a chance to regain momentum and fewer believe that this would be anything but a stopgap for a future reckoning.

Israel's plan is to delay that reckoning by periodically invading and bombing Palestinians into oblivion. Israel's plan is to traumatize a nation so that their submission becomes the only way out. War crimes trial or not, the powers that count on the global scene have little appetite for international law governing their decisions. During the Gaza war, even with late condemnation of some of Israel's air strikes, America kept providing Israel with arms and munitions. This was true for the United Kingdom as well. Any leverage with regard to Israel was given away at that moment and, of course, that assurance had to have been given in advance. Should it only be Israel brought up on war crimes or should the United States and the United Kingdom be brought to the The Hague as well?

The reckoning has to include international actors like the United Nations, the NGOs that serve the Palestinian people and the churches that have spoken out during this emergency and at difficult times in the past. They all have failed to protect the Palestinian people and their moral outrage has fallen on deaf ears. Or rather, their moral outrage has been shared around the world – to no effect. Condemning Israeli actions, calling for the enforcement of international law, invoking our common humanity and seeking the protection of God, again all have failed. With Gaza soon to be rebuilt – once again – and life there to be resumed under some form of blockade and occupation – once again – resuming life as it was, under the same code of conduct and with the same appeals, condemns Gaza and Palestine in general to the cycle of occupation, violence and invasion. After Gaza, it is time to ask whether the United Nations, the NGOs and the churches aren't enablers of Israel's occupation and Palestine's demise.

It can be at times that one's investment in humanitarian work runs against the very goals humanitarian work seeks to attain. Arguing for rights while being dependent on Israel for approving personnel and protecting property may in actuality trump the mission itself. Even the fierce debate on divestment that the Presbyterian Church conducted right before the invasion – a debate that BDS supporters won by a handful of votes – was shadowed by the refusal of the church to sacrifice anything for the solidarity they professed. Just over a hundred million dollars of divested stocks were at issue while the overall portfolio of the church is in the billions.

And, let it be said, even the supporters of the BDS resolution emphasized over and over again that the divested stock would not cause a loss in the churches portfolio. Commitment without sacrifice doesn't go very far. Soon after the BDS victory, Israel was in Gaza and the Presbyterian Church fell silent. When it did speak out it was in the broadest of international law generalities.

No matter the course that war crimes against Israel takes over the next months, Palestinians and their supporters should understand that these paths are only levers in the attempt to get Israel to somewhat loosen its overall control of Palestinian population centers in the West Bank and Gaza. This is the sad truth about BDS as well – a truth that its supporters, including Ilan Pappe, either don't understand or are reluctant to speak in public about. BDS should be seen as a lever, like international law, to loosen Israeli control. For the moment that control is loosened or appears to loosen, the United States and Europe will move to protect Israel and offer some form of Palestinian autonomy. There is no way, no matter what Israel does, that the nation-state powerbrokers will abandon Israel as a state or discipline it in a manner that allows real Palestinian freedom.

Thus while the calls for action, like this YWCA - Palestine call, are strong, they are rear-guard actions. They are levers to restrain Israel's domination not forge Palestinian freedom:

> *This is five year old Hajar Muharram. Look into her eyes. She is from Beit Lahya, one of the towns where the residents were forced to evacuate their homes due to bombing. Her family got one of those courtesy missile knocks on the roof telling them they had 58 seconds to leave. Hajar and her family of seven fled their home and have since joined hundreds of other Palestinians taking refuge in a United Nations school which is being used as a shelter. But shelters are not guaranteed safe places; over 8 UNWRA schools/shelters have been bombed. Look into her eyes for this may be the last time if her school is targeted.*

> *Children are bearing the brunt of this newest offensive military bombardment. Since July 8, over 430 children have been deliberately killed in Gaza with over 2,878 more injured. In addition there are over 373,000 more who require psycho social support. There is no post traumatic stress syndrome*

because the trauma is ongoing. If Hajar survives she will be one more child in need of this support. Look into her eyes and see what has happened to her home or neighborhood.

Over 485,000 people have been forcibly displaced which is almost one third of the Gaza population as a result of Israel's latest military offensive against Gaza. Many of them were refugees from 1948 or have grown up in one of Gaza's refugee camps. Their homes in the camps have been targets. Hajar in Arabic means "emigrated" but there is nothing voluntary about her displacement. The legal term for this is forced transfer. The term on the streets is ethnic cleansing.

We believe that the international community has the legal and moral responsibility to protect the Palestinian population living under Israeli occupation and that it must hold Israel accountable regarding its severe violations of international humanitarian law. Lack of accountability will continue to fuel Israeli atrocities and crimes.

We must move past moral outrage to direct action to demand Israel to end collective punishment of civilians. This is the year of solidarity with Palestine. Stand with us and stand up to Israel's impunity. In addition to ending this military occupation against the State of Palestine here are things you can do:

*   **Call** for a durable, comprehensive and mutually agreed upon ceasefire agreement which secures facilitation and access to humanitarian aid and opening of borders to and from Gaza; lift the siege on Gaza;*

*   **Call** for Palestinian leaders and UN Security Council to refer the situation in Gaza to the Prosecutor of the International Criminal Court (ICC);*

Support *the YWCA's advocacy project Fabric of Our Lives which supports refugee and internally displaced people's rights including the Right of Return;*

Join *the worldwide BDS movement as a tool for accountability and ending impunity especially sanctions like weapon and trade embargos.*

Join Forces to End this Occupation

Who can deny this plea and the rational, legal and moral argument found within and outside of the lines? For those who seek justice, the plea is unassailable. But the world powers rarely think ethically, they think geo-politically. Translated into politics, the ethics contained in the Y's action alert become limited.

What about the other enablers of this assault on Gaza, those who through word and lobbying encouraged the invasion of Gaza and vilified those who tried to stop it? The list is long and includes people from various backgrounds. It includes barely known columnists and international luminaries. It includes the noted Holocaust survivor, Elie Wiesel.

If truth be known it includes an overwhelming number of Israelis and Jews around the world. It includes Jewish identity that now embraces a violence rarely embodied by Jews in history. Violence is defining us as a people. It is defining what others think of Jews around the world.

Today, when people hear Holocaust, they think Gaza. This is less about comparing the two events – such a comparison trivializes the innocent victims of the Holocaust and the innocent victims of Gaza. Rather, the image of the Holocaust correctly cautions people around the world that the suffering of innocents is to be avoided and opposed. To do what Israel did in Gaza – ostensibly in the name of protecting Israel against a Hamas-led Holocaust – is to appropriately call Jewish symbols to the fore. It is to call Jewish history to account.

The Jewish issue is not only about Israel. It is about the garnering of Jewish resources – philanthropy, religious and intellectual – toward the projection and enabling of power. After the Holocaust, the issue of Jewish empowerment came to a head and appropriately so. But soon that empowerment was being used for more than self-protection. After Gaza, we know where that power has led Jews. While Jews should be afforded some kind of independent Jewish empowerment, the type and scope of Jewish empowerment has been called into question. It is an issue in need of deep consideration.

Such consideration represents a beginning. Jews have chosen to symbolize their empowerment in the state of Israel. For better and worse that state will remain and be defined as a Jewish state. Yet as in other states, the majority of the state's population hardly controls the policies of the state. World Jewry has even less to say about Israel's policies.

The issue is simple yet endlessly complex. The state of Israel claims to speak and act on behalf of all Jews – yet the vast majority of Jews have little or nothing to say about Israel's domestic and foreign policies. Even the Jewish establishment in the United States that supports Israel has little or nothing to say about what Israel does and does not do. Yet Jews are increasingly defined within the context of Israel's actions.

During Israel's invasion of Gaza this rings true. In France, Germany and elsewhere in Europe increasing number of anti-Semitic incidents are reported. In some cases Jews are targeted because they are Jews. Even in progressive movements, at least on the fringes, anti-Semitism can be found. Though these incidents rarely threaten Jewish life and in no way resemble aspects of the horrific past in Europe, the rise in anti-Semitism testifies to a deep ambivalence about Jews on the world stage. Israeli policies exaggerate this ambivalence but it would be foolish to see Israel as anti-Semitism's sole cause.

Nonetheless, it is for Jews to chart our own destiny.

What is that destiny? Could it be that after a long history of contribution and suffering Jews are destined to become conquerors, building and maintaining a modern-day Sparta?

After Gaza, it seems likely this will be the road taken.

Some say that such a view as I take is a political and organizational downer. It might lead to apathy and thus encourage Israel and prolong the suffering of Palestinians. But the remedies offered that are less than honest and, for now, unrealizable, create an illusion of progress where none is found.

After Gaza, the truth hurts. It has to. It is only when we come together in that truth that a way through might be found. Such a way will not be found now and when it is found it will be too late. Jews know this lateness all too well.

Kirk Douglas
The Vikings

LOOKING
FOR THE PALESTINIAN KIRK DOUGLAS

The ceasefire did not hold or was allowed to lapse so Israel and Hamas are at it again – asymmetrically. "After the ceasefire before the next ceasefire" is another form of politics. The families of Palestinians who die during this political dueling should be so advised.

As in: "Your loved ones died so we could continue to negotiate the next round of suffering. Thank you for your service to our great cause."

During the ceasefire several diplomatic initiatives were announced. The United Nations declared it was willing to oversee the building of Gaza once again. That was the carrot.

The UN's stick? This would be the last time. Which means that if Israel destroys Gaza once again, it will be left as it is.

Should Israel see this as a threat? A threat that forces it to sign on the dotted line?

The European Union's proposal is more detailed. Reportedly the EU is offering Israel a way out of the Gaza situation by, among other things, opening a route for Gazans to travel and trade through Cyprus.

Cyprus is an intriguing option. It's Europeans thinking out of their box. Or it's Europe thinking European-style.

Is Europe trying to solve the Israel-Palestinian impasse through Europe or at least on the border of Europe?

What Gazans want is an open border with Israel and Egypt and a real connected Palestinian state with East Jerusalem as its capital. Perhaps another time.

Think of the difference in power and hope. Germans provide Israel with submarines that are then nuclearized by Israel. The European Union wants to placate Gaza – and Israel – with a sea corridor through the Mediterranean.

I doubt Gazans will travel by nuclear submarines. Perhaps they will travel by wooden boats protected by Viking-era, European Union, warships.

Thinking thusly, my mind wandered to the 1958 movie, *The Vikings*. Many hope that the Palestinians will come up with their version of Nelson Mandela – the Palestinian Mandela. Perhaps they would be better served looking for the Palestinian Kirk Douglas.

Diversion is the name of the game. The international community wants the slaughter stopped. The international community doesn't want to do the heavy lifting necessary to accomplish this goal.

One can't afford to be cynical. There's way too much suffering. With the international "actors," however, a little satire might save the day.

Lest Gaza be left in ruins the next time – as it is today.

Standing for Justice
Scotland

BOYCOTT ISRAEL?

It could be any street in Israel - Jerusalem, Haifa or Tel Aviv. Israeli soldiers guarding the public. Israeli soldiers even protect those who come from afar to serve Palestinians in Jerusalem and the West Bank.

Ironic isn't it? To be guarded by those who transgress those one has come to serve. Even during Israel's invasion of Gaza.

The globalized world of massive suffering and service to those in need is rarely simple. Development and humanitarian aid to Palestinians is no exception.

After all, those who work for the UN, NGOs and the churches are protected, investigated and censored by the Israeli government. Their movements in and out of Israel are monitored and controlled by the Israeli government.

The question of questions was broached years ago but now in the wake of Israel's invasion of Gaza – at this moment of reckoning – it needs further consideration. Do humanitarian and development workers serve the Palestinian people – only? Or do they, in an important way – also – serve the interests of the Israeli government?

It isn't direct service to Israel as in a corporate welfare model. Humanitarian and development workers can be crucial to the survival of individuals and communities in need. They may function as witnesses to the humanity of the suffering. They can also function as humble enablers, siphoning off the steam of occupation and invasion.

Perhaps Marx was right about religion and thus by extension humanitarian assistance, the religion of choice of many in our modern secular age. Are religion, development and humanitarian aid opiates for suffering Palestinians and especially for the world community that washes its hands of the situation as long as children aren't burning?

Even the prophetic denunciation of Israeli power, as some NGOs and churches have properly engaged in lately, can serve the same function.

The UN, NGOs and churches have to face the question of questions: Should they continue to serve as they have with the results obvious to all or contemplate a boycott of Israel, withdrawing their personnel, aid and services? Concentrating on an occupation and blockade that for all intents and purposes are permanent has failed.

"Boycott Israel" wouldn't go over big in most quarters. Perhaps it shouldn't even be put on the table. It's difficult to draw a red line when the needs of the people you're serving are so great.

This would be upping the stakes considerably. Boycotting Israel might not work either. But if you've noticed, the needs of Palestinians keep becoming greater. And greater. Each year. With no end in sight.

The international community is outraged – and does nothing.

Serving the disenfranchised is rarely simple. Especially when under the auspices of the Jewish state. So UN, NGO and church business as usual during and after Israel's invasion of Gaza?

Perhaps there's no other choice. The UN, NGOs and the churches may be trapped like the people of Gaza.

Yet where there's no way out, a way out still has to be found.

What is that way?

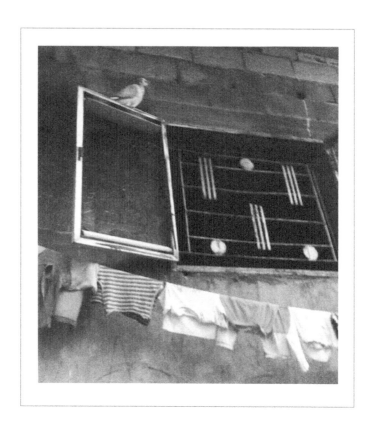

Ahmad's Bird

Gaza

KNIGHT
IN SHINING ARMOR?

Well here it is, a Gaza ceasefire proposal that is circulating widely. Would it be worth waiting for?

The *Times of Israel* is reporting the proposal and, if it is agreed upon, some Jews and Palestinians will celebrate their version of victory.

Reading the proposal, I can see how some Jews and Israelis might celebrate a signing. For Gazans, who are struggling to survive Israel's onslaught, a sense of relief would be palpable. But looking carefully at the text, the central issues of the Israeli-Palestinian conflict are unexamined, let alone resolved.

Here is the reported text:

> *Israel will halt all attacks on Gaza – by land, air or sea. There will be no ground incursions into Gaza.*
>
> *All Palestinian factions in Gaza will stop all attacks against Israel by land, air or sea, and will stop the construction of tunnels from Gaza into Israel.*
>
> *The opening of crossings between Israel and Gaza – the passage of people and goods will be allowed in order to rebuild Gaza. The transfer of goods between Gaza and the West Bank will be permitted, according to principles which will be determined between Israel and the Palestinian Authority.*
>
> *Israeli authorities will coordinate with the PA all issues of funds related to Gaza and its reconstruction.*

The elimination of the buffer zones along the security fence in the northern and eastern Gaza Strip and the deployment of PA forces in those areas beginning January 1, 2015. This will be conducted in several steps: At first the buffer zone will be reduced to 300 meters from the border, then 100 meters and finally the removal of the buffer zone altogether with the deployment of PA troops.

The fishing zone off the Gaza coast will immediately be extended to 6 miles, and will be gradually extended to 12 miles, in coordination between Israel and the PA.

Israel will assist the PA in rebuilding infrastructure destroyed in Gaza, and will assist in providing basic necessities for those Gaza residents who were forced to flee their homes due to the fighting. Israel will provide medical aid to the wounded, and will expedite the transfer of humanitarian aid and food through the crossings.

The Palestinian Authority in coordination with Israel and international aid groups will provide the basic products needed to rebuild Gaza, according to a predetermined schedule which will allow those driven from their homes to return as soon as possible. Egypt implores the international community to provide swift humanitarian and monetary assistance for Gaza's reconstruction, according to a set schedule.

Upon the stabilization of the ceasefire and the return to normal life in Gaza, the sides will conclude their indirect negotiations in Cairo within a month after signing the deal. The exchange of prisoners and bodies will also be discussed at that time.

The possibility of constructing an airport and sea port in Gaza will be considered in accordance with the Oslo accords and other previous agreements.

Nowhere in the text is the issue of Palestinian nationality or statehood affirmed. It isn't even mentioned. The international community is called upon and Egypt – whose fascist dictatorship is receiving accolades for their involvement in the process – implores the world to help with the reconstruction of Gaza. But the overriding importance of the proposal is the consistent appearance of Israel and the Palestinian Authority as a team. They lead the way for Gaza's return to the human zone of life abundant.

Perhaps.

"In coordination with Israel and the Palestinian Authority" – that's the order of the day. Funds, rebuilding, the movement of goods, it's quite nice to see how the parties, bitter internal and external enemies, are now to work closely together.

Of the ceasefire points, here is my personal favorite: "Israel will assist the PA in rebuilding infrastructure destroyed in Gaza, and will assist in providing basic necessities for those Gaza residents who were forced to flee their homes due to the fighting. Israel will provide medical aid to the wounded, and will expedite the transfer of humanitarian aid and food through the crossings." A beneficent Israel it is. Or an Israel that has its hands in everything Palestinian. And profiting politically and economically from the whole affair.

Taking in the wounded and helping to feed the hungry is a plus. Helping those who just weeks, even days earlier, you made homeless, injured and killed – should this be held up as a creative and reconciling plan? To avoid war crime tribunals?

For those who wanted Israel punished, this possible truce doesn't begin or end there. It's almost as if nothing happened. The slate is wiped clean.

Perhaps this is a trial balloon but soon we will find out.

Amazingly, Israel could emerge from such an agreement as a knight in shining armor.

Who would have thought?

Trails of Terror
Khuza

WITNESSING GAZA

As we approach the endgame of this phase of Gaza's tribulations – for rest assured, Gaza's tribulations will continue – reporters on the ground are writing and photographing the disaster. Like all of us, they're looking for hope in Gaza's ruins. They're not finding much.

Among these reporters are Jews from Israel and America. They're observing what their fellow reporters are – devastation as far as the eye can see. They're meeting with the grieving, the homeless and the injured. They're also finding out what the dead look like close up.

I'm thinking especially of young Jews like Max Blumenthal, whose twitter photos are arresting, and Allison Deger's incisive reporting. But there are others, like the veteran Israeli reporter Amira Hass. In the coming days, more Jewish reporters will arrive.

I have never seen the devastation of war. It can't be easy for any of the reporters. Is it different for Jews?

A few of these reporters have been in touch with me. They are startled and shaken by what they're experiencing. Israel's invasion seems pointless. What they see is the sheer brutality of it all. Since this might be the point of the invasion, asking the deeper questions of life and death is natural.

Like all of us, they're struggling to make sense of suffering – as human beings and as Jews. The Jewish identifier is intriguing, especially since most of the Jewish reporters aren't religious and have tenuous, if any, connections with the larger Jewish community. They think of themselves as typical reporters and photojournalists. Most don't want to be singled out as Jews. They just "happen" to be Jewish.

But most of the Jewish reporters are not well-paid journalists assigned by the higher-ups for the Gaza beat. It's volunteer duty, raise your own money and take the risk.

Still the soul searching may have been unexpected. To one who wrote, I offered that as a human being she is witnessing part of the human drama without blinders. Being Jewish adds another dimension:

> Yes, the most obvious thing you're doing is helping the world know what happened in Gaza and encouraging solidarity with the Palestinian people. But, as well, you are a Jew observing what "we" have done – Israel specifically and Jews around the world who enable Israel's violence.
>
> Has Jewish history come to this? What are Jews of Conscience like you to do with what you are seeing, touching, experiencing?
>
> You are a different pair of Jewish boots on the ground. First the soldiers, now you. You might not know what to do with this. I don't know either. Who does? Jews have never descended to this level of depravity before.
>
> The end of Jewish history as we have known and inherited it – I think that's what you're witnessing. Whatever ethical values were present in our tradition – what both of us consciously or subconsciously draw upon – are gone.
>
> Like – or with – the Palestinians – Jewish ethics have literally been blown away. What you write, the photographs you post, detail this end.
>
> Documenting the end isn't easy – I think it's very, very important.
>
> There is no return to what is lost. This may pain you in a way that isn't definable. I think of you as experiencing a trauma that comes from another place and is now inside you.

That trauma isn't going away – I think you know that. It will get worse. That's what I read in your words. I see it in your photos.

If only there was something hopeful I could share with you. Nothing in my lifetime – perhaps in yours since you are much younger but I also doubt this – will set this aright. Barring a strike from the heavens – a miracle of sorts – Palestinians will remain under Israel's thumb.

We need clear-headed political and economic analysis – your reporting demands this – and something more – your reporting demand this as well.

That something more is within and beyond your personal/reporting/solidarity journey. You are witnessing a horror that is present-day but resonates with the Jewish past. It's defining our Jewish future.

Yes, you're witnessing our future in Gaza – which has already arrived. So in my mind you're a witness – a witness at the end. Small comfort.

Hold fast – what you're doing is important.

Jewish boots on the ground in Gaza. First Israel destroys, then Jews and others detail the end.

Of course, Gaza remains alive and this, too, must be written about and photographed. And these Jewish reporters are alive, too. Which is a source of hope. Perhaps I should include this hope when the next email from Gaza arrives.

These Jewish boots on the ground are a sign of hope – the only hope we have – at the end. So I have to choose my words wisely.

I also have to tell them the truth as I see it. It wouldn't be right to condescend to those who bear the weight of Jewish history as it comes to its end.

Jews of Conscience
United States

THE
JEWISH PROPHETIC
COMES HOME

As the various ceasefire collapsed, the United Nations muddled and the European Union scrambled – all diversions from the real issues at hand in Gaza –Jews of Conscience were on the march. Though prohibited and harassed by organized thugs, Jews marched in great numbers in Tel Aviv. Across the United States, dissenting Jews organized and made their outrage known.

Demonstrations occurred in Washington, D.C., in Chicago and other cities across America. In Philadelphia, a group of Jews of Conscience occupied the offices of the Jewish Federation. Rabbi Rebecca Alpert described the scene:

> On Friday morning, August 7th, 40 activist Jews, most under the age of 35, went to the offices of the Jewish Federation in Philadelphia, and prayed there. Ten members of the group held a civil disobedience action inside the Federation building. There they were the first Jewish Voice for Peace chapter to deliver a petition signed by over 35,000 supporters, urging the Federation and other Jewish leaders to take a public stand not just for an immediate ceasefire, but for an end to the underlying conditions of siege that makes life unbearable for Palestinians in Gaza. They demanded–and received–a meeting with the Philadelphia Federation CEO, Naomi Adler. While they waited, refusing to leave the building for over four hours, they sang Jewish songs of peace. Outside, a crowd of supporters read poems, sang songs of peace, and read the names of almost 2,000 people who have been killed in Gaza these past three weeks. In the end, six protesters were removed from the building in handcuffs.

117

Why did they do this act of civil disobedience? Alpert continues in almost a liturgical cadence:

> *These people are part of the growing number of American Jews who have done similar actions in cities across the United States, including New York, San Francisco, Seattle, Washington D. C. and Boston. They are sickened by the carnage being wrought by the state of Israel, a state that claims to be a Jewish state, and which therefore speaks in their names. They find that they can no longer stand idly by; can no longer remain silent.*
>
> *They needed to recite the names of these 1800 dead human beings to remind the leadership of the American Jewish community that these 1800 dead were human beings and not human shields as the Israeli government demeaningly refers to them.*
>
> *They needed to recite their names to remind American Jews that unless we speak up and protest we are complicit in these deaths.*
>
> *They needed to recite their names because the continuation of a cease fire does not open up the ports of Gaza, or allow freedom of movement for its residents, or allow free import of food and medical supplies.*
>
> *They needed to recite their names to tell the world that not all Jews agree with what Israel is doing now, or has been doing for the last 47 years of illegal occupation of Palestinian lands.*
>
> *They needed to recite their names to let Israel know that there are American Jews who believe that political actions have consequences, and that Hamas, with its ugly, violent and desperate measures did not attack out of anti-Semitic hatred* but because of Israel's ongoing blockade of Gaza that has crippled their economy and reduced the land to poverty.

They needed to recite their names to tell the leadership of the Federation that Jewish money would be better spent on the sick and poor in our city than on funding Israel Solidarity rallies.

They needed to recite their names to remind all of us all that every life is precious.

Jews have been on the frontlines of dissent for decades so Jews arrested for civil disobedience is hardly unusual. But this is different. In the Civil Rights and South African apartheid eras Jews protested against American foreign policy in consort with official Jewish organizational policy. Now Jews occupy the offices of important Jewish organizations protesting against Israeli policies and those institutionally affiliated Jews who enable these policies and stifle Jewish dissent. In previous times the Jewish prophetic voice was turned outward - on behalf of others. Increasingly it is turned inward – on behalf of others.

After Gaza, the Jewish prophetic is returning home. As with the ancient Jewish prophets, Jews of Conscience, as Jews, are critiquing injustice committed and enabled by Jews. Jews of Conscience are demanding the end of Palestinian suffering and Jewish assimilation to militarism and war. They risk what the ancient prophets risked: being labelled anti-Semitic and self-hating.

When Biblical prophets are read, usually we select passages supportive of issues and sentiments we want to highlight. Often the prophetic hope of return to justice – and therefore to God - is emphasized. But a fuller reading of the Biblical prophets shows an utter disdain for injustice. The Biblical prophets have a scorched earth punishment – for Jews – when Israel continues to stray.

The prophetic indictment is delivered with an unprecedented and unrelenting moral outrage. Practicing injustice, Israel is turning its back on God and its own destiny. The prophets cannot abide this false turning. They deliver a condemnation, amazingly included in Jewish holy texts, that is without parallel in other religious or political literature.

119

Should it then be a surprise that such a deeply rooted justice-seeking is reawakening among Jews around the world as Israel, by any secular or religious standard, so flaunts morality and ethics?

This was Rabbi Irving Greenberg's great fear. After analyzing the impossibility of speech about God in the face of the burning children of the Holocaust, he offered a way out through the rescue of burning children in the present. Only then could we begin to think again about God. But what if the state of Israel violates that very rescue and instead burns children in the name of its security?

With the prophetic so deeply ingrained in Jewish history and identity, Rabbi Greenberg knew that Jews would struggle to accept the state of Israel's actions as an (almost) normal state. In Greenberg's view, Jews and the state of Israel remain different – both are called to a higher ethical standard. In an age of Jewish empowerment, however, an empowerment that Greenberg believes is mandated by the Holocaust, Jews have to acknowledge perfection is impossible. Like any state, Israel acts in untoward ways that will deeply disturb Jews immersed in the Jewish ethical tradition. However, Greenberg feel that Jews have to stay the course, understand the post-Holocaust situation of world Jewry and fend off those outside and within the tradition that cannot stomach the complexities of normalization.

Rabbi Greenberg rightly feared the application of the prophetic to Israel's actions. What would become of the state of Israel if it was called to account by the Jewish prophetic?

For Rabbi Greenberg, after the Holocaust, the Jewish prophetic has to take a back seat to Jewish empowerment in the state of Israel. Prophetic judgment is too harsh for any state. If applied to Israel, it might weaken or unintentionally help others destroy it. Thus Greenberg places Jewish dissenters on Israel on notice. Unintentionally, critique of Israeli policy toward Palestinians might lead Jews into a second Holocaust.

With Jews undergoing the process of normalization, the stakes are high. With Rabbi Greenberg, many Jews feel that the Jewish prophetic has to be quieted.

For many years, Rabbi Greenberg's understandings held sway. Though there has been Jewish dissent throughout the last decades, for the most part it has remained in the background. The leaders of the Jewish community have kept a tight rein on the internal workings of the community, censoring and disciplining Jews who speak out on behalf of Palestinians. Yet it is becoming clear. The Jewish community's control is weakening.

With the Gaza war, has the tide turned? If it has, in what direction can Jewish dissent move? Surely, there can be no return to a time when Jews were completely vulnerable to surrounding communities whose intentions and symbolic structures were deeply ambivalent, if not downright hostile, to Jews and Jewish interests. Yet the assumption of Jewish power in Israel has gravely impacted Palestinians in a negative way. It is making it more difficult, if not impossible, for Jews to uphold Israel and be faithful to the ethical tradition Jews inherit.

Perhaps Jews should declare the inheritance of the prophets to be null and void, wipe the prophetic slate clean and join the Other Nations with aplomb. After the struggles and suffering of Jewish history, including the Holocaust, it makes sense. Why bother with the ethical scruples of the prophetic tradition when a Middle East empire is at the fingertips of the Israeli military?

The question of questions that Israel's invasion of Gaza raises in the bold strokes of the prophetic.

Is the Jewish prophetic up to the task at hand? Can it join with the prophetic from other communities to become a joint front for peace, justice and reconciliation in Israel-Palestine? Or will it continue to be a small blip on the radar of Jewish and other powers?

The history of the Biblical prophets does not bode well for the Jewish prophetic that is exploding in our time. For the most part, the Biblical prophets bit off more of Israel than they could chew. The result was that Israel continued on its way while the prophets suffered ridicule, accusations of betrayal and violence. Israel also suffered exile from the land and untold misery.

In the Bible, the prophets were commissioned by God and God looked after the prophets – at times. Especially when the prophets were in the deepest of trouble, God was often silent, absent, AWOL. And today, after the Holocaust, Rabbi Greenberg is right that neither Israel nor her prophets can call upon God.

Yet the Jewish prophetic continues on regardless of the silence of God and the admonishment of the Jewish establishment. That hardly signals victory. What it does tell us is that a civil war within the Jewish community has arisen. After Gaza, the Jewish prophetic remains.

For the Palestinian people, the Jewish prophetic returning home is too late. Nonetheless, hope is alive wherever the prophetic appears.

As so often in human history, the prophetic appears late – and right on time. This offers Jews and others in solidarity with the Palestinian people and Jewish history another chance to choose a different path.

After Gaza, that path is fraught with untold suffering.

ABOUT THE AUTHOR

Marc H. Ellis is retired University Professor of Jewish Studies and Director of the Center for Jewish Studies at Baylor University.

He is the author and editor of more than twenty books including *Toward a Jewish Theology of Liberation, Unholy Alliance: Religion and Atrocity in Our Time* and, most recently, *Future of the Prophetic: Israel's Ancient Wisdom Re-Presented.*

Professor Ellis's writings have been translated into more a dozen languages and he has lectured around the world. Currently he is writing an almost daily commentary series, *Exile and the Prophetic*, which can be found at mondoweiss.net.

NEW DIASPORA

New Diaspora, founded by Marc H. Ellis, is committed to providing a communications platform that enables a broad range of voices to tell their stories in a variety of formats.

Professor Ellis serves as the editor, working closely with each project as it moves from concept to publication.

If you have a story to tell, an experience, poetry, art, photography, prose, historical or fiction . . . we would like to hear from you.

We offer professional design, layout, and support for the projects that we publish.

We look forward to reviewing your manuscript or a summary of your concept.

Please connect with us at newdiasporabooks.com for more information.

We look forward to hearing from you.

Building Community . . . one cup at a time

retail | wholesale | training

bethlehemcoffee.org

NEW**DIASPORA**
B O O K S